the
Truth
about
You

the
Truth
about
You

Remembering
Who You Are,
Where You Came
From, and Why
You Are Here

Bradford Baber

gatekeeper press™
Tampa, Florida

The Truth about You: Remembering Who You Are, Where You Came From, and Why You Are Here

Published by Gatekeeper Press
7853 Gunn Hwy., Suite 209
Tampa, FL 33626
www.GatekeeperPress.com

Image on page 149 from: Phil Degginger / Alamy Stock Photo, Image ID Number: AARDBG

Library of Congress Control Number: 2023937013

ISBN (paperback): 9781662937163
eISBN: 9781662937170

For truth seekers everywhere _ _ /

...especrally Marsha!

Table of Contents

Introduction

I want to know God's thoughts; the rest are just details.[1]
—Albert Einstein

THIS BOOK IS ABOUT *YOU*. HERE YOU ARE OFFERED THE CHANCE TO *remember* a remarkable *truth*, which you brought with you into this world but have most likely forgotten. This is your golden opportunity to embrace, once again, how truly extraordinary you are. Perhaps, on some deep level, you already know this to be true.

Since you found your way to this book, you might already be following a path of self-discovery, searching for genuine answers to life's most basic and compelling questions:

- *Who am I?*
- *Where did I come from?*
- *Why am I here?*

You're in luck. Because here you will rediscover the true answers to these three vital questions, thus revealing the deeper meaning and purpose of your life. As a truth seeker, what lies ahead for you is the road to regaining your awareness of how each part of your *true* human anatomy—*soul, body,* and *mind*—converge to become the amazing being that is *you*, and how these three vital parts of you come together to create your entire life experience. On this path, you will rekindle an essential truth which you already know at the core of your being: that you are *whole, complete,* and *perfect* just as you are. This is the truth that

1. Ronald Clark, *Einstein: The Life and Times* (London: Hodder and Stoughton Ltd., 1973), 33.

will set you free. This is the nirvana, the Tao, the *rebirth,* or *salvation* that, as a truth seeker, has been your longtime quest.

I admit, this journey will be trying at times. The ideas you will encounter here are, by themselves, not difficult, nor are they new. However, you will undoubtedly run across new ideas that will challenge your prior ways of thinking. So, brace yourself. My aim is to make these concepts comfortable and accessible to everyone, even the busiest and most casual of truth seekers. The whole idea here is that the truth is not as complicated as it might seem. It is decidedly self-evident and should not require long, drawn out explanations.

The good news is that remembering *who you are, where you came from,* and *why you are here* does not require years of study, painstaking research, strenuous pilgrimages, attending a church, seeing a shrink, or going *anywhere* to get *anything.* The truth about you is available right here, right now, patiently awaiting your rediscovery.

About Me

I have always been fascinated with how the parts of a whole fit together. As a child, my toys were maps, house plans, building blocks, outdoor fortresses, and the like. While playing, I loved connecting the parts, observing their relationships, and assembling them to create something bigger. In adulthood, these pastimes naturally gave way to more practical endeavors, such as organizing a closet, arranging a drawer, making a "to-do" list, drafting an itinerary, or planning a project. Watching the parts come together meaningfully and purposefully to form a whole has always exhilarated me, especially when my attention turned to the more esoteric facets of life.

Life's meaning and purpose, and other philosophical and metaphysical questions, first captured my attention as a teenager, probably because at that time I was coming to terms with being apart from the "norm" as a young gay man, grappling with love and relationships in that context—especially my relationship to god. My budding self-awareness fit nicely alongside my passion for relating the parts to the whole. In this case, I was relating the *part* that was me to my place in the *whole* universe.

In my early forties, true to my nature, I decided to write a book describing how all fields of human knowledge were somehow interrelated, inevitably pointing toward one simple, unified, whole truth. This personal *theory of everything* was an ambitious undertaking and, after months of work, such an imposing mission began to feel tediously academic and awkwardly disingenuous. So, I stopped.

Several years later, while on a routine plane trip, something remarkably simple and powerful happened to me. Relaxed, earbuds streaming my playlist, and apparently unusually receptive to recognizing the truth, I became intensely aware of the chorus to a familiar song chanting the words "mind, body, and soul." For some reason, in that moment, I understood: *it really is just that simple.* These are the true, essential parts of all of us. I was captivated by their utter simplicity and began asking myself: How do these parts fit together? Where do they come from? What do they do? What is their purpose?

Inspired by this event, I began to write again. This time my writing felt authentic and meaningful. I was connecting the dots, uncovering layers, and discovering more parts all pointing to the *truth* about: *Who am I? Where did I come from? Why am I here?* I was beginning to remember. Now I was filled with a heightened sense of purpose. I recalled that the three basic parts of the whole me—soul, body, mind—connected me to all human beings everywhere, as if we were one. I also realized how much more fulfilling everyone's life experience would be if we could all just remember this truth. I was inspired to tell everyone what I had remembered.

But who would listen to *me*? How could I possibly find an audience to share these profound connections I had remembered? Besides, who

The Truth About You

was I to presume I had arrived at anything special? The problem of having no professional writing experience was further complicated by a notable lack of drama in my life. I had never faced down any catastrophic, life-altering, or otherwise transformative event compelling me to remember what I had previously forgotten. There had been no critical illness, nervous breakdown, sporadic homelessness, debilitating trauma, or major upheaval of any kind in my life leading me to this truth. My life has been ordinary. As I write this, my two feet are planted firmly and quite unremarkably in a regular job, with a typical family, normal friendships, ordinary hobbies, and a traditional focus on building a nest egg. But as is sometimes the case, out of the ordinary comes the extraordinary, if you allow it.

I am *no one* and, at the same time, I am *everyone*. I simply had to pay attention. I believe the same is also true for you. While I hope the message of this book resonates with you, in the end, you should not listen to me. Instead, you should listen to *you*. That is the whole point of this book.

Listen to You

I hate to admit that I am a neglectful reader. Rather than devote time to the noble pastime of reading books, I usually turn to the voice inside me to get to the truth. I am a much better "producer" of information than a "consumer" when it comes to books, television, social media, and so on. This idea of information *production* versus *consumption* was recently the focus of publisher and best-selling author, Dawson Church, in his book *Mind to Matter,* in which he discussed the creative nature of best-selling authors:

> Most people are passive. They take information in. They listen to the radio, watch shows and movies, and read the occasional book. They are consumers of information rather than producers of information. They are constantly influenced

4

by the information they are consuming. When it comes to best-selling authors, the flow of information tends to run the opposite direction. They are much more interested in the information they can produce than what they can consume. They are active producers of information rather than passive consumers of information.[2]

In today's world, it is hard to resist compulsively consuming information because there is so much of it screaming for our attention. We are truly in an age of information overload with television, internet, text messages, and social media streaming and teaming to grab our focus. As Edward O. Wilson, known for his contributions in ecology, evolution, and sociobiology, tells us: "We are drowning in information, while starving for wisdom."[3]

This book is different. Here, we are all about *producing* information. It is about *you* listening to *you* as the highest and best source for what is important and true. I hope that as you pay attention, you will come to remember how all the parts of one, simple, spectacular truth fit together, beginning with the most spectacular part of all: *you*.

Old and New

The ideas within these pages are not necessarily groundbreaking or earth-shattering. For the most part, it is all old news. Much of what I say here has already been said countless times. It can be traced throughout human history, across a multitude of cultures, in ancient writings, religious scripture, scientific studies, contemplative psychology, philosophy, and new age thought. What *is* new is how these ideas are

2. Dawson Church, *Mind to Matter: The Astonishing Science of How Your Brain Creates Material Reality* (Carlsbad: Hay House, 2018), 28.
3. E.O. Wilson, *Consilience: The Unity of Knowledge* (New York: Alfred S. Knopf, 2000), 294.

stitched together to offer you a comprehensive, integrated, and simple approach to what is important and true in your life. My hope is that it will resonate with you and help you to fully remember the astonishing truth about *who you are, where you came from,* and *why you are here.* A truth that is remarkably simple.

To be sure, it is not *all* old news for you in the upcoming pages. There are several new ideas along the way that will challenge your current thinking and open your mind. Of course, these are explained in the upcoming chapters, but they include:

- trusting your innate wisdom in favor of learning from the "experts"
- adopting an integrative "parts to whole" approach to get to the truth of life's meaning and purpose
- envisioning a sacred new *human* geometry that puts you at the center with a *u-axis* connecting you to all points surrounding you
- recognizing a human anatomy that focuses on your true essential parts: *soul, body,* and *mind*
- embracing your personal connection to the divine, even if you currently do not believe in such an idea
- practical advice on how to use what you have remembered along the way to create more contentment and well-being in your life and the world around you

Shoshin—Beginner's Mind

As you begin this journey of remembering I will ask that, from this point forward, you trust your intuition and let go of any preconceived ideas. Like a curious child, remain open to the possibilities and available to the experiences that await you here, especially your internal experience—wherein *you* listen to *you*. This open and receptive approach is known in Zen Buddhism as *shoshin*. A term meaning beginner's mind.

There is tremendous value in cultivating a beginner's mind. In his notable book *Zen Mind, Beginner's Mind*, Zen master Shunryu Suzuki explains: "In the beginner's mind there are many possibilities, but in the expert's mind, there are few."[4] He suggests that there is a danger that comes with expertise. Our "expert" tendency is to block information that contradicts what we have previously learned in favor of information that confirms our present view. We might think we are learning, but in fact we are just skimming through information looking for something that substantiates our current beliefs and behaviors. Most people do not want new information, they want validating information. With a beginner's mind we let go of our preconceived notions and look at every aspect of our life as if for the first time—with awe and wonder.

An open-minded shoshin approach is the best way to remember what your mind wants to forget. As you proceed here, let yourself be a witness to the "give and take" that occurs in the dialogue between the judgmental boundaries of your mind and the creative vision of your soul. They are both your allies. Think "outside the box." Consider the possibilities and challenge the limitations. In this way, we evolve as human beings and as a whole humankind.

Sati—Mindfulness and Meditation Practices

If you have ever explored Buddhism, you might be familiar with mindfulness meditation. In Buddhist teachings, mindfulness is the seventh step of the *Noble Eightfold Path* (right view, right resolve, right speech, right conduct, right livelihood, right effort, right mindfulness, and right union) and the first of *Seven Factors of Enlightenment* (mindfulness, investigation, energy, joy, tranquility, concentration, calmness). In sacred Pali and Sanskrit texts, the word *sati* was used to convey the idea of mindfulness. But sati originally had a deeper and

4. Shunryu Suzuki, *Zen Mind, Beginners Mind* (Boulder, Colorado: Shambhala Publications, Inc., 2020), Prologue

more nuanced meaning. In this 2005 interview, American Buddhist monk, Bhikkhu Bodhi, put it like this:

> The word ["sati"] derives from a verb, *sarati*, meaning "to remember," and occasionally in Pali sati is still explained in a way that connects it with the idea of memory. But when it is used in relation to meditation practice, we have no word in English that precisely captures what it refers to. An early translator cleverly drew upon the word mindfulness, which is not even in my dictionary. This has served its role admirably, but it does not preserve the connection with memory, sometimes needed to make sense of a passage.[5]

The meaningful historical connection between *mindfulness* and *remembering* is significant for our purpose here. It is one thing to read about an idea and understand it intellectually, and another to grasp it experientially. It was Albert Einstein who said that "the intellect has little to do on the road to discovery. There comes a leap in consciousness, call it intuition or what you will, when the solution comes to you and you don't know how or why."[6]

In this book, mindfulness exercises are provided at the end of each chapter to stimulate the act of your remembering. These short "sati" practices are intended to *experientially* breathe life into an important truth in each chapter so that you are not merely thinking about the concepts, but instead *becoming* them. According to David Lynch, the renowned film director and creator of the David Lynch Foundation for

---

5. "Interview with Bhikkhu Bodhi: Translator for the Buddha," *Inquiring Mind* 22, No. 2 (2006): http://www.inquiringmind.com/article/2202_w_ bodhi-interview-with-bhikkhu-bodhi-translator-for-the-buddha/.
6. "*Forbes* Quotes: Thoughts on the Business of Life," *Forbes*, Accessed February 17, 2023: https://www.forbes.com/quotes/173/

Consciousness-Based Education and World Peace: "The thing about meditation is: You become more and more you."[7]

Finally, as you proceed here, be patient. Remembering is a process. Trust the journey. The ideas you encounter here will likely resonate along the way but may not entirely fit together until after you have taken the full journey, just like life itself.

Now it is time for you to listen to you.

Now it is time for you to remember.

---

7. David Lynch Foundation, "The thing about meditation is, you become more and more you."—David Lynch. Facebook, May 9, 2016. https://www.facebook.com/DavidLynchFoundation/photos/a.175572862467475/117925 2585432826/?type=3

(1)

Remembering

A man went in search of fire with a lighted lantern.
Had he known what fire is, he could have cooked his rice much sooner.
—Zen parable

THIS IS YOUR STORY. HERE, *YOU* ARE THE PROTAGONIST, THE HERO, AND the star. What unfolds here is the truth about you: who you are, where you came from, and why you are here—a truth you have carried with you since you entered this world but have since forgotten. It is this *forgetting,* yours and that of others, that is the cause of all the trouble and suffering in the world. *Remembering* is the cure. So, here, from chapter to chapter you will be deeply remembered, plainly understood, and genuinely appreciated for all the special qualities that make you an amazing human being. Isn't that ultimately the simplest and most authentic key to your well-being—to be seen and valued for who you truly are?

If you think this sounds like a lot of bunk and twaddle, then I urge you to read on; your persistence through any skepticism will be rewarded. Because you are about to rediscover the *remarkable* truth that you are far more awesome than you have ever imagined.

Remembering this truth is very empowering, so be careful what you wish for. I advise you to read this book only if one or more of these statements pertains to you:

- You contemplate the meaning of life—especially your own life.
- You want to discover your life's purpose.
- You seek clarity on what really matters in this world.
- You struggle with understanding and developing meaningful relationships.
- You wonder if there is a god and, if so, what is this god like?
- You feel inspired to do great things with your life.
- You believe that you might have some special talent or superpower to share with the world.
- You are increasingly aware of the connection between you and all others.
- You worry whether you, your family, community, or planet is safe for the future.

Does any of this sound like you? If so, this book is a great opportunity for you. If not, then this might not be the right time for you yet. Not to worry. It will be here for you when you are ready.

How Did You Forget?

You will probably agree that many of life's most profound mysteries and compelling questions appear on the list above. You might even believe that the list represents what is most *important* in life. Getting to the *truth* of them all, or even just one of them, might seem like a tall order for such a short book. But this journey is genuinely all about getting to the heart of what is *important* and *true*. And it is all simpler than you might expect.

Skeptics will say that, even if it was possible, it would take tremendous effort to get to the bottom of what is important and true. They will grumble that this book speaks with absolute certainty about questions that can be answered only after a lifetime of transcendent spiritual practice, a religious epiphany, or following years of study and research culminating in some radically new scientific proof. While these criticisms might seem valid at first, my response is very simple. It truly is all about *you*. *You* are the *practice*. *You* are the *epiphany*. *You* are the *proof*. All you must do is remember what you already know.

How is this possible?

First, contrary to anything you might have been told, you truly are extraordinary. You arrived in this world as a tiny human being with a vast awareness and pure understanding of *who* you are, *where* you came from, and *why* you are here. With this awareness and understanding came absolute clarity about what is undeniably important and *true* in this world, what you might even call the *meaning* and *purpose* of your life.

Then, shortly after you arrived, and before you had the opportunity and the capacity to share this infinite wisdom with your new, human tribe—*oops*—you forgot. As a newborn, infant, toddler, and child, during the normal process of growing up and adapting to the world, you became distracted, first by your remarkable new human body, and then by all the human drama that surrounded you. Amid all these distractions, you quite literally forgot *who* you are, *where* you came from, and *why* you are here. You forgot the truth about you.

This process of forgetting is well documented in the field of neuroscience. David Eagleman, well-known neuroscientist and *New York Times* bestselling author, puts it this way:

> The process of becoming someone is about pruning back the possibilities that are already present. You become who you are not because of what grows in your brain, but because of what is removed. As we grow and learn new skills, we reduce the number of [neural] connections in our brain in favor of focusing on a smaller number of stronger connections. As you learn to read squiggles on a page, the connections go from being universal to being specific. Those links you don't use, you lose. Over the course of childhood, brain circuitry

13

is wired up according to experience and interaction with the environment.[8]

So, after we are born, we sacrifice a huge degree of the innate cosmic wisdom that we brought with us into this world in order to hang on to the more mundane and useful information we need to assimilate and grow up. This is the science of forgetting.

The story of forgetting and remembering—*your* story—has been told countless times over the centuries in the themes of mythology, folklore, literature, and film. One celebrated example is the classic American film *The Wizard of Oz,* based on the book *The Wonderful Wizard of Oz* by L. Frank Baum. In the climactic scene toward the end of the film, after an extraordinary adventure in Oz that culminates with the annihilation of the wicked witch, Dorothy and the Scarecrow ask for the help of Glinda the Good Witch so that Dorothy can return home to Kansas:

Dorothy: Oh, will you help me? Can you help me?

Glinda: You don't need to be helped any longer. You have always had the power to go back to Kansas.

Dorothy: I have?

Scarecrow: Then why didn't you tell her before?

Glinda: Because she wouldn't have believed me. She had to learn it for herself.[9]

Dorothy had to *remember.* No sdivne!

Like Dorothy, you are having an amazing adventure that seems very real to you. Your life is filled with your own version of "lions, and

---

8. The Brain with Dr. David Eagleman, "What Makes Me." Directed by Dan Clifton, Catherine Gale, and Johanna Woolford Gibbon. Aired October 21, 2015, on PBS.

9. Noel Langley, Florence Ryerson, and Edgar Allen Woolf. "The Wizard of Oz." Film script,(1939).

tigers, and bears," wicked witches with flying monkeys, and special tasks that call upon your "brains, heart, and courage" along the way. Life in your version of Oz is full of challenges that can seem insurmountable, especially when you have forgotten the truth of who you are.

The characters you encounter along your yellow brick road have unwittingly conspired to perpetuate your forgetfulness. Rarely do they intend harm, but because they are often just as forgetful as you, and immersed in their own version of Oz, their behavior can sometimes seem mischievous or, at times, even malevolent, showing up anywhere from the insensitive comment of a friend or colleague to the injurious acts of a stranger. As a result, it is likely that you—like the tin man, the scarecrow, and the lion—have subscribed to the illusion that your human nature is, to some degree, heartless, dimwitted, and fragile, and that you are "less than" and separate from all other human beings and, most certainly, from any god in whom you might choose to believe. The colorful characters in your story, who sometimes play the role of parent, teacher, faith leader, or employer, among others, have told you that there are certain deeds you must perform, tasks you must undertake, or something special you must prove in order to succeed in life. You have been required to follow rules, practice atonement rituals, and "play the game," in order to be worthy of acceptance, honor, and love. And if you do all this, you might qualify for your trip back to Kansas or whatever your personal version of "heaven" looks like. Amid all this drama, you lost touch with the truth—you forgot how wonderful you already are.

But all is not lost. Just as the Good Witch Glinda arrived on the scene in a magic bubble to help Dorothy, there is a bubble of good fortune appearing for you, right here, right now. Because here you have an opportunity to reconnect, once again, to the vast intelligence that accompanied you into this world, just by listening to you and remembering what you already know. This innate wisdom has always been, and still is, with you. It quietly and gently whispers for your attention to remind you who you are and what is important and true in your life. The whisper comes in many forms: a song, a story, a work of art, a walk in the woods, a chance encounter, a life-changing event, and so on. But you must pay attention so as not to miss it. This book is one such whisper. Fortunately for you it is a rather loud whisper.

What is Remembering?

By now you are probably wondering how remembering works. How do you remember who you are, where you came from, and why you are here?

Ordinarily, *remembering* refers to the act of bringing to mind an awareness of something or someone you have experienced in the past. This could even mean the recollection of past life experiences if you believe in reincarnation. But I define remembering as a process more like what you might call "connecting the dots." Here, remembering refers to an integrative approach to the truth that occurs by recognizing how each part of the truth fits together and rolls up into the whole. The definition we will use is:

> The process of recognizing a vital, but forgotten, truth, arising from a renewed awareness of how its integral parts relate to the whole.

In this book, the parts that we focus on are your *soul, body* and *mind*, which are the fundamental components of every human being. You might even think of these three parts as *members of the whole* you, whom you are reconnecting, rejoining, or *remembering*.

When you remember how each of these elemental parts of your being combine, relate, and cooperate, the truth of *who you are, where you came from,* and *why you are here* comes to light. Then all the other pieces of what is important and true begin to fall into place. At first it might feel like you are learning these ideas for the first time;

however, remembering is not exactly learning. We *learn* perfunctory facts, whereas we *remember* fundamental truth. Learning is a function of the analytical mind, which is just one part of you. It ignores the other two essential parts of your being—body and soul—which are necessary for the expansive awareness and understanding that comes with remembering. You might catch your analytical mind saying, "Sorry, I don't get it. I just can't remember." But if you stick with it, and keep an open, beginner's mind, the truth will ultimately resonate with you. This is because you have really known it all along. You are simply remembering what you have forgotten.

Fundamentally, remembering is a rediscovery or realization of who you are. It is an awakening, of sorts, that some might call *enlightenment*. However, for most people, enlightenment implies the attainment of some knowledge or understanding that you *do not* have rather than a reconnection with a truth you already possess. What I mean here by remembering is not an act of *becoming*, but of *returning to*. Because of this subtle and important distinction, and because, for many people, the word *enlightenment* is associated with other established philosophical or metaphysical doctrines, in this book I use the word *remembering*.

An Integrative Approach

The "parts to whole" focus of remembering is, by its nature, an *integrative* approach to the truth. In fact, the words *integrative* and *integrate* come from the Latin word *integrare*, meaning "to make whole" and are also at the root of *integrity*, which implies the state of being unified, whole, complete, and one.

Integrity has played a significant role in my life. Growing up in Indiana, my small country high school participated in a program known as Hoosier Boys State, in which rising male seniors are nominated by faculty for an off-campus experiential learning program with the goal of learning about the state's political process and teaching future leadership skills. This opportunity, sponsored by the American Legion, is presented as "a week to shape a lifetime." I was honored to be picked for the selection process, which required me to write an essay and complete a personal interview. During my interview, one of my examiners asked me: "What does integrity mean to you?" I went blank. I had heard this word before. I knew it was something good. But for the life of me, I could not come up with a definition or an example.

That year I was chosen as the runner up, or "alternate," from our school and did not attend Boys State. I have no idea to what extent my inability to articulate an understanding of integrity played in that decision, but that interview, and the word *integrity*, have been etched into my memory ever since. You could say that integrity continues to play a significant role in my life, as I integrate that experience with the process of remembering who I am.

Whether you realize it or not, *integrity* has great significance for you too.

Throughout this book, we will break down the parts of the whole truth for you. This approach helps restore your memory of how the soul, body, and mind *integrate* as one, and bring an understanding of what is important and true, just as they did when you entered this world. Although you have come to rely on your mind and body for most of your awareness and understanding, by re-engaging your soul you are better equipped to remember everything you brought with you into the human dimension, in particular the whole, forgotten truth of who you are, where you came from, and why you are here, in other words, the meaning and purpose of your life.

This approach to remembering can also be said to be integrative because it draws upon the established views of many diverse disciplines to point to a whole, unified truth about who you are and how you are connected to the world around you. Here, we look at Eastern and

Western perspectives, scientific and religious doctrine, physics and metaphysics, psychology and philosophy, as well as literature and fine arts in order to deconstruct old walls and build new bridges among these separate towers of wisdom. The result, you might say, is a simple and tightly woven "theory of everything."

What's In It For You?

It may surprise you to discover that your life is not as complicated as it seems. What's going on here is really quite simple. All the parts of your life fit together perfectly and work just as they should. But "the devil is in the details." You routinely get lost in all the minutia and the drama of life and, consequently, lose your perspective, forget who you are and how you are connected to the whole, big picture. This predicament shows up in your life in countless ways.

- worrying that your best friend is mad at you and not raising the issue directly
- joining a coworker in "stirring the pot" at the office over a recent new hire
- getting dragged into the gossip mill with friends at dinner before getting the facts
- becoming fixated on social media hype or an agitating news story
- making a foolhardy expensive purchase with the underlying belief that it will enhance your personal worth
- assuming that a friend's intentions are negative before giving them the benefit of the doubt

This is just a tiny sample of the countless ways minutia and drama can pull your focus from what is important and true in life.

As I have said, most of the world's problems, big and small, are caused by human beings forgetting who they are. The compass that points us toward personal contentment and well-being is out of alignment simply because we have forgotten what is important and true. Now is the time to remember the common denominator that unifies us all and makes us human so that we can make choices that prevent needless, unintended harm to ourselves, our relationships, and the living planet we inhabit. The true answers to the important questions of *who you are, where did you come from,* and *why we are you here* are remarkably the same for all of us. Remembering these answers is the key to transforming the world into a more habitable place of well-being for everyone.

When it comes to life's biggest questions and toughest challenges, it is time we had some clarity. Human beings suffer from the delusion of separation from one another. We are so intently focused on the things that differentiate us, that we literally forget to acknowledge, and even stop looking for, the ties that bind us. This blunder, and the resulting suffering, is the underlying cause of most of our personal and social *dis-ease,* from the illnesses of our individual bodies and minds, to more global and systemic afflictions, such as starvation, social unrest, and environmental degradation.

Remembering the truth about you brings a new, *integrated* perspective to your life. It reveals the true, simple, underlying order of the seemingly complex and chaotic world. It allows you to see the *big picture,* and what is important and true in your life. Here is what is available to you when you can remember:

- recognizing how all the parts fit together and how life really works
- realizing the simple meaning and purpose of your life
- enhancing your personal contentment and well-being
- answering life's biggest questions and navigating your toughest challenges
- transforming your world into a more habitable and user-friendly place

- making choices that create a more joyful and fulfilling experience for you and everyone

You deserve a more joyful and fulfilling experience of life. You really do.

As you journey through this book and begin to remember who you are, you will discover the very good news—the comforting truth—that ultimately, in the grand scheme, everything is going to be okay. You are always safe. You cannot fail in this life. Try as you might, you cannot screw it up, even if you believe you already have. This might be contrary to everything you have been told throughout your life. Remembering this truth is like a warm blanket, always there to comfort you.

This is what's in it for you.

If you have read this far, you are probably ready for a warm blanket. Maybe you are also ready to hear the loud whisper of this book and begin your extraordinary journey to remembering the truth about you. Good, because you are well on your way.

Up to now, I have talked a lot remembering the *truth* and what is important and *true*. Needless to say, the focus of this journey is the *truth* about you. So now is a good time to take a deep dive into what is exactly meant by the truth—*the whole truth*.

Sati One: The Whole Breath

If this is your first time practicing mindfulness meditation, *welcome*. If you are already familiar with meditation, then it is a return to some basics. At the beginning of each sati exercise, I will ask that you "find your seat." Steps 1–5 below describe what this means. Refer to these five steps again, as necessary, in the upcoming sati exercises.

1. Find a quiet place where you will not be disturbed for about 10–12 minutes.

2. Take a relaxed seated position that works for you. There is no "right" way, just *your* way. Just be sure you can sit comfortably, still, and alert. Feel free to experiment. For example, you might:

   - sit with your buttocks on the floor or on a yoga cushion, legs crossed however you like

   - kneel with your legs folded underneath your buttocks, perhaps with a pillow or cushion added for comfort and support

   - sit upright in a favorite chair, feet on the floor, hands by your side or on your lap

   - assume a lotus position, if you are familiar and comfortable with this

   - use the "legs up the wall" position (my personal favorite) by laying on your back with your legs extended up the wall, in an "L" shape, and your buttocks a few inches from the wall. In this position, I like to elevate my lower back with a cushion under my sacrum.

3. As you relax into your seat, scan your body and release the tension in locations where you hold stress, such as the brow line, jaw, shoulders, stomach, and hands.

4. Read through the following exercise steps to become familiar with what you will be doing.

5. Then gently close your eyes and keep them closed during the practice, opening them as necessary to refer to the exercise instructions again.

6. After settling into your seat, begin by taking a deep breath, hold it for a count of three, then release it slowly. Do this three times, pausing briefly between each breath. If comfortable, place your hand on your belly to feel its rise and fall as you breathe.

7. Return to your breath's normal rhythm.

8. With your eyes still closed, for the next few breaths, begin to focus your attention on the inhale and exhale of your breath.

9. Using a shoshin beginner's mind, spend a minute or two imagining what it must have been like as a newborn to breathe for the first time. For example, you might ask yourself:

    Am I doing this intentionally, or is it happening to me?

    Is it soothing or troubling?

    Is the movement of my breath smooth or uneven?

    In which parts of my body do I most feel my breath?

10. Next, return your attention to the present moment. Follow your inhale, and notice the very slight pause at the top of your inhale before your exhale.

11. Similarly, at the end of your exhale, observe the pause before you begin to inhale.

12. Do this a few times, and use your beginner's mind to become curious about both pauses.

    Have you noticed these before?

    How long does each pause last?

How does each one feel?

What happens if you shorten or extend them?

Can you identify subparts to each pause?

13. Set a watch or timer for two minutes and, with your eyes closed, breathe normally, and focus your awareness on each of these four parts of your breath, noticing how they relate, connect, and integrate to form a complete breath: (1) inhale, (2) pause at the top, (3) exhale, (4) pause at the bottom.

14. Finally, relax your awareness and open your eyes.

Congratulations. This was an opportunity to bring awareness to something that is essential to your life but often goes unnoticed or is taken for granted. Breath awareness is a common mindfulness technique. Most people think of the breath as having two parts: inhale and exhale. But in this exercise, you saw that the breath is more intricate than you might have realized. Each part of your breath has its own unique attributes, and each plays a vital role in your breathing. In fact, without each part, you could not breathe.

You were likely aware of these parts of your breath when you first entered this world and began to breathe for the first time. But as you grew up, you had many more things competing for your attention, so breath awareness just faded into the background. Breathing just seemed to take care of itself without you paying much attention to it. We will use breath awareness often in these sati exercises since it is a handy and effective teacher on this journey.

(2)

Truth

Truth is singular. Its versions are mistruths.[10]
— Davis Mitchell, *Cloud Atlas*

AN OATH OF SWORN TESTIMONY IS COMMONLY USED IN THE COURTS OF many countries to oblige a witness to attest to the facts in a legal proceeding. For example, "I swear to tell the truth, the whole truth, and nothing but the truth, so help me God." When taking such an oath, the witness is expected to tell the truth, as he or she knows it to be.

But just what is the truth?

How do you know what is true?

Since you have found your way to this book, you are most likely interested in the truth. As a *truth seeker,* you are looking for answers to life's important questions. You are trying to piece it all together in a way that makes sense. You already know that getting to the truth of anything can be a daunting task. Getting to the truth of it *all* certainly seems impossible for one human lifetime.

Why is the truth so obscure? Perhaps because, even though the fundamental nature of truth is quite simple, it is viewed from so many different angles and expressed in so many different ways that the path to truth can be baffling. So, if you are on the path to truth, you must be

---

10. David Mitchell, *Cloud Atlas* (Random House Trade, 2004), 5.1.2.

very clear about how to recognize it when you encounter it. That is the purpose of this chapter.

Truth: A Cultural Perspective

You are not alone on your quest for truth. Human beings have long grappled with the obscurity of truth. In ancient Rome, for example, it was believed that the goddess *Veritas,* the embodiment of truth, was so elusive that she hid herself in the bottom of a holy well. Throughout the ages, the mystery and meaning of truth has been ardently pursued by scholars, philosophers, and theologians on all continents. Today, in your own pursuit, if you googled "truth," you would find various websites discussing the *epistemological* theories of truth, such as *correspondence, coherence,* and *pragmatic.* You might also stumble across another branch of philosophy known as *metaphysics*, which relates to truth by focusing on the ultimate nature of reality.

Suffice it to say that how *you* get to the truth, and what *you* believe to be true, is largely based on the cultural influences at play throughout your life. Generally, this means either an Eastern (*Asian*) or Western (*European*) slant on truth.

The Western point of view has its roots in Greek philosophy, the Age of Enlightenment, and the Protestant Reformation. It assumes that a god, or perhaps a pantheon of Greco-Roman gods, created absolute truth, and that this truth is seen in the laws of science and nature. From the Western perspective, the path to truth is outside of you and is proven either by empirical investigation or by contemplating the relationship between man and god (or gods). The Western perspective focuses on getting to the truth by thinking the "right" way, that is, logically, rationally, or morally. If you are a Westerner, you most likely prefer to trust the research or rely on your pastor, priest, or rabbi to clarify what is true, even though, ironically, the scientific and religious perspectives often conflict.

In an interesting and often-cited *American Psychologist* study[11], Westerners were shown to be more likely to adopt an Aristotelean approach to truth, known as the "Law of the Excluded Middle," which states that if two people disagree, only one can be right and the other must be wrong. In other words, a statement cannot be both right and wrong.

In contrast to the West, major Eastern views of truth originate from Buddhism, Taoism, Confucianism, and Hinduism. These belief systems do not agree on the existence or nature of god (or gods), and so the notion of divine truth is much less important than in Western thought. At the heart of Buddhism are the "Four Noble Truths," which encourage the acceptance of the world "as is" and offer a plan for coping with humanity's inevitable suffering.

Lau Tzu, founder of Taoism, taught that the *Tao* (path or road) is the way of nature and ultimate reality. Tao is often described as the force that flows through all life. A happy and virtuous life is one that is in harmony with the Tao and with nature. From an Eastern point of view, all events in the universe are interconnected. Truth is a *given* and does not have to be proven. It is simply revealed through the circular patterns of its eternal recurrence.

The Eastern perspective downplays the need to *think* about what is true, and sometimes even suggests that you stop thinking altogether. It asks you to search inside yourself and experience unity with the universe through stillness, mindfulness, and meditation in order to perceive what is true.

In the *American Psychologist* study cited above, Easterners more often get to the truth by applying a principle of Confucianism known as the "Doctrine of Mean," which holds that if two people have opposing

11. K. Peng and R. E. Nisbett, "Culture, dialectics, and reasoning about contradiction," *American Psychologist,* 54, no. 9 (1999): 741–754. https://doi.org/10.1037/0003-066x.54.9.741

viewpoints, the truth must lie somewhere in the middle. Both sides are partly right and partly wrong.

These two dissimilar and culturally biased approaches make getting to the truth far more complicated than it needs to be. Because of their notable differences, many casual truth seekers have come to believe that the truth is just like the Roman goddess Veritas—hidden and unknowable.

One Truth, Many Versions

It is fair to say that, as human history has unfolded, two present-day "champions" of truth have emerged: *science* and *religion*. These two rivals have long vied for ownership of truth, seeking answers to life's basic questions—*who* you are, *where* you came from, and *why* you are here—by applying either scientific methodology or religious contemplation, within both Eastern and Western cultures.

Consider, for example, the age-old questions of *creation* versus *evolution*, or *pro-life* versus *pro-choice*. Collectively, scientific and religious thinkers have produced numerous lenses from which to view these, and many other, controversial topics: pragmatism, logical positivism, coherentism, naturalism, relativity theory, quantum theory, materialism, idealism, rationalism, scholasticism, Catholicism, Protestantism, Taoism, Buddhism, Judaism, agnosticism, atheism, and the list goes on. The intellectual campaign for truth naturally becomes very mind-centric, neglecting the more direct, holistic, and integrative—soul-body-mind—pathway to truth. In the end, it produces way too many contradictory and confusing versions of truth, proving again how we can get lost in the weeds, forsaking (yes, *forgetting*) the natural grasp of truth that we held when we entered this world.

Amid all this ambiguity, perhaps you have arrived at what you call "your personal truth" and, consistent with this view, you believe that there are as many versions of truth as there are people in the world.

Although this is a very popular and democratic view of truth, authentic truth is not the least bit democratic. Truth is a benevolent dictator. There is only one truth. What might seem to be many individual truths are merely the different interpretations and experiences of one simple, singular, common truth.

To illustrate this point, imagine a large collection of beautiful cut crystal vases lined up on a long table. Each vase has its own unique and magnificent pattern. You fill the first vase with water. You look through the vase to observe the water, but you can see the water only through the unique pattern of the vase. Then you pour the water from the first vase into the second and look at it again. It appears different to you now because this time you are seeing it through a different pattern of glass. You continue this exercise until you have observed the water from the perspective of each of the vases. Throughout this exercise, the water has remained constant, only its container has changed.

The vases are like all of us—each one *unique* and *magnificent*. The water is like *truth*—stubbornly constant.

The Nature of Truth

Truth *is* the water of life. It permeates and shapes our world. It universally and inescapably saturates all that is, even when it is not yet proven by scientists, proclaimed by prophets, or remembered by you.

Truth is the foundation, and the "common denominator," of all that you experience. Thankfully, it is quite simple to describe because, as truth seekers, we must be precise about what it is we seek. Even more important, we must be clear about what we mean here as we examine the truth about you. To that end, see if this definition resonates with you. Truth has two defining qualities. For something to be true, it must be both:

- *constant,* and
- *constructive*

As the ever-present *constant*, truth never pauses, fluctuates, or changes. It is *always,* meaning that truth is, quite literally, fixedly present in *all ways*, at all times. It is invariably and inescapably *universal*. It is everywhere. Nothing and no one is exempt from the certainty of truth. In terms of space and time, truth is both *infinite* and *eternal*—endless and forever. It has no beginning or end. Truth simply "is," always has been, and always will be.

To be *constructive* here means that truth is the elemental, underlying organizational principle, or *construct*, of all that is, whether seen or unseen, accepted or not. It is the *essential foundation* and *structural order* of all that you experience and have yet to experience. Truth holds it *all* together and, ultimately, makes perfect sense amid seeming chaos and confusion.

Does this definition of truth feel right, seem reasonable, and fit with your experience? If so, then it is a sign that you are beginning to listen to you and remember what you already know instinctively, at the most profound, cellular, subatomic, and energetic level of your being. In other words: you know truth "in your bones."

The Crusade for Truth

Truth reveals the perfect symmetry and balance of everything. You can think of truth as the "program" that is running in the background of your life. It both encompasses and transcends science and religion, putting an end to their passionate rivalry once and for all. It is the *real* reason behind all scientific reason, the *first* "cause" of all cause and effect, and it is the *source* of all spiritual and religious inspiration. Although we might invent different versions of the truth, in doing so, we are simply eyeing the same unassuming, constant, and constructive target, merely from different perspectives and through individual filters. These *perspectives* and *filters* are our beliefs, but what we believe is not necessarily true.

The grand significance of our many dissimilar beliefs is that, collectively, they underscore the *unity* in our thirst for truth. We all know *constant and constructive* is out there, somewhere. We just want to get to it. While our perspectives and methods might vary, we are all still part of a common crusade: to remember what we already know.

Satyagraha—Truth Force

As you might expect, truth is quite powerful and compelling all on its own. When confronted with the brute force of truth, it is hard to deny it. You only need to pay attention to it when it whispers or, in some cases, startles you like a bucket of ice-cold water poured over your head.

In a recent *Chicago Sun-Times* podcast, retired *Apollo 8* astronaut, Jim Lovell, recounts his impactful brush with truth while looking back to the earth from space and observing how "it appeared to me that God had given mankind some sort of a stage to perform on, and how the play turns out is really up to us."[12] In this instance, Lovell simply paid attention to his experience in order to remember the truth of the connection between two parts of the whole: mankind and god, a connection we will explore in the next few chapters.

In another example of the power of truth, the introduction to this book tells of my encounter with the incontrovertible truth, coincidentally while also mid-flight, as I remembered that all human beings are essentially the sum of three basic and important parts: soul, body, and mind. This glimpse of truth was the genesis of the book you are now reading.

The intrinsic power of truth was given a name in 1906, during the Indian independence movement, when Mahatma Gandhi coined

12. Robert Herguth, "Face to Faith, Episode 5, Jim Lovell." *Face to Faith* audio podcast. March 23, 2018. *Chicago Sun-Times*, https://chicago.suntimes.com https://soundcloud.com/user-485806571-926828048/face-to-faith-episode-5-jim-lovell

the new Sanskrit word: *satyagraha*. It is formed from *satya* (truth) and *agraha* (insistence) and has come to mean *truth force*. Satyagraha is important for you here because, as you move through these chapters, you may very well be compelled by the utter force of truth to reconsider existing thought patterns and view certain aspects of your life very differently. Ultimately, along your path of remembering, the *force of truth* will reveal how the *true* parts of you—soul, body, and mind—integrate and work together in ways you might never have considered before. Remarkably, Gandhi sometimes referred to satyagraha as *soul force*, accentuating the soul's important role in recognizing the truth.

Gandhi's conception of satyagraha influenced many other notable thought leaders around the world, including Martin Luther King Jr.'s civil rights campaign in the United States in the 1960s, and Nelson Mandela's struggle to end apartheid in South Africa in the 1990s. These transformative movements underscored the reality that satyagraha moments are not always comfortable, but when they point you toward the undeniable truth, they can be profoundly transformative. On your journey to remembering here, you are likely to experience several wonderful *aha!* moments of truth or, in this case, satyagr-*aha!* moments. Maybe you already have.

Oath of Truth

May the "truth force" be with you. Satyagraha! My pledge for this journey is to tell the truth about you, the *whole* truth, and nothing but the truth. Ironically, to get to the whole truth, we must first look at a very conspicuous *untruth*. It is the great illusion. The illusion of *polarity*.

Sati Two: Thought Clouds

1. Find your seat (refer to Sati One, if needed) and take a moment to get settled.
2. Begin by taking a slow, deep breath, hold it for a second, then release it with a gentle but audible sigh. Notice the sensation in your body as you release your breath. This type of breath is called a "cleansing breath," or sometimes a "sounding breath."
3. Take two more cleansing breaths, then return to your breath's normal rhythm. Notice how you feel after that short breath exercise.
4. Now, with your eyes still closed, focus your awareness on your breath's natural inhale and exhale. Observe how effortless your breath is, almost as though you are being "breathed," instead of you breathing. Spend another minute in this awareness.
5. It is normal for the attention on your breath to shift to your passing thoughts. Sometimes, thoughts are even racing through your mind. Allow yourself to accept that this will happen, because it will. When it does, gently return your focus back to the rhythm of your breath.
6. As you are breathing, spend about two minutes observing the theme of your thoughts as they pass through your mind, as if they were clouds floating through the sky. What are you thinking about?
   > *Worried about doing this correctly?*
   > *Distracted by a sound or sensation?*
   > *Focused on some future event?*
   > *Planning what you will do next?*
   > *Reflecting on a past experience?*
   > *Solving a problem?*

7. Spend as much time as you like with this, then relax your awareness and open your eyes.

Just as your breath has more than one part, so does mindfulness meditation. Mindfulness is *not* the experience of emptying your mind of thoughts, as many people believe, because you cannot do that. It is the *practice* of returning your attention from your interceding thoughts back to your breath over and over again and accepting that this is the natural two-part rhythm between breath and thought in meditation. As you meditate, allow yourself to notice your thoughts coming and going in your mind, as if they were puffy, white clouds passing though the blue sky.

3

Polarity

We Don't See Things As They Are, We See Them As We Are.[13]
—Anais Nin

WE LIVE IN A VERY SPECIAL TIME AND PLACE. FOR THOSE OF US WHO are truth seekers, the world we live in, although deeply fascinating, is also irrepressibly confusing. This is largely because in our absurd, nonsensical world, which I call the *human dimension*, the only way for us to experience something is by comparing it to whatever it is not. Only through the "is-is not" relationship between two *polar* opposites can we comprehend them both.

This condition equally applies to our experience of the truth. For us to fully comprehend what is true, we must also consider its opposite. In doing so, we compare what is true to what is *untrue*, or *illusion*, and consider how each relates to the other. This act of comparing the "is" to the "is not" is embraced universally by both Eastern and Western approaches to truth. Take for example the Tennyson quote: "Tis better to have loved and lost, than to have never loved at all." Regardless of whether you get to the truth of this proposition by applying the Eastern "doctrine of mean" ("better" may lie somewhere between "having lost love" and "having never loved") or the Western "law of the excluded

---

13. Anais Nin, *Seduction of the Minotaur,* (Athens, GA: Ohio University Press,1961), 124.

middle" (it is either "better" to have loved or it is not), both rely upon the comparison between whether it "is" or "is not" better to have loved. In the human dimension, whether you take an Eastern or Western stance, truth exists only relative to what is untrue. This is the way of *polarity*. And this is where you get your first glimpse of the truth about you—by looking at what you are *not*.

It might surprise you to know that you are already an expert on polarity. Whether you realize it or not, you use polarity as a tool every day to experience the world. You put on a jacket when it is *cold* outside to feel *warm*; or you flip the light switch in the *dark* to *brighten* a room. In every moment you experience "is-is not" and make choices based on the relationship between the two. In the human dimension, you are unquestionably a master *polarist*. But before we move too fast into the specifics of your natural proficiency with polarity, it will help you to first understand exactly what is meant here by the *human dimension*.

The Human Dimension ("HD")

As a human being, you are well acquainted with the world inhabited by humans. It is the place where we all live, meet up, and interact with one another. It is our "common ground," where we focus our attention and direct our energy. It is comprised not only of planet Earth, but all the other planets and heavenly bodies in space as far as our awareness can reach. It encompasses all that we experience as physical objects and beings, as well as the non-physical or *metaphysical* space and energy that surrounds us, for instance light and sound. On this journey of truth, this realm is called the *human dimension*, or "HD" for short. You are about to see why *dimension* is an appropriate choice of words for this place.

The reason for calling this dimension *human* is that everything that appears and disappears in the HD is the product of our individual and collective human choices. It is the *human* dimension because it is the *human* beings who are in charge, calling the shots, and setting the agenda.

One simple but striking example of this uniquely human capacity is the ongoing recovery of endangered species, previously on the verge of extinction, but now thriving again due to the collective choices made by human beings with initiatives such as the Endangered Species Act (1973) and various zoo conservation programs around the globe. These actions have boosted the populations of Aleutian Canada Geese in California, American Crocodiles in Florida, and Grey Wolves in the Rocky Mountains. On the flip side, the Weather Channel recently reported that three bird species—the Spix's Macaw in Brazil, Alagoas foliage-gleaner in Brazil, and the Po'ouli in Hawaii—are now classified as extinct due to man-made deforestation, indicative of a collective human choice, albeit involuntary, to create a future world without these animal species.

These examples show how human beings can shape the human dimension at the macro level, but you and all human beings are equally in charge at a more personal level as well, as you manufacture your individual experience of the HD in every moment. Exactly how you do this is described in the upcoming chapters.

The notion that it is human beings who create the HD might be a new and potentially unsettling concept for you. It could also be a *satyagraha* moment. You may not be quite ready to accept the idea that you have the power to create the world around you, let alone the entire human dimension, because with such power would undoubtedly come tremendous responsibility. Yet, in truth, you are a creator. The HD is a virtual hotbed for your creation. You create in every moment of every day. And you do it all with the tool of *polarity*.

The Nature of Polarity

The word "polarity" comes from the Latin word *polus*, meaning "near or relating to the Earth's poles." *Polaris,* the brightest star in the Ursa Minor constellation, has the same name origin. Polaris is also known as the "North Star" because it lies in a direct line with the axis of the Earth's rotation, right above the North Pole, seemingly motionless in the sky. For this reason, Polaris has been used as a navigational sign by seafarers and explorers throughout history. Similarly, polarity is your means for experiencing and navigating the human dimension. Thus, it is important to have a firm grasp on how polarity works.

I define polarity in terms of five basic elements:

1. A thing may enter your awareness only in the presence of its opposite.
2. A thing is understood only by comparing it to that which it is not. It is the relative difference, or *value*, between the two that allows you to know both.
3. Only through polarity may you have experiences in the HD.
4. Polarity is an illusion because, by its own definition, it exists only relative to that which it is not.
5. That which is *not* polarity is *absolute.* (The *absolute* is described in the next chapter.)

How does this description sound to you? Although you have never heard it defined this way before, it likely makes sense to you because you have worked with polarity ever since you entered the HD. It is as natural and effortless for you as the inhale and exhale of your breath, which, incidentally, is an excellent example of polarity.

You experience *light* only in contrast to *dark.*

You understand *up* only relative to *down.*

You move *left* only in comparison to *right.*

You know what is *wet* only having felt *dry.*

You are *happy* only because you have been *sad*.

You sense *pleasure* only because you have faced *pain*.

Polarity is so crucial to your experience of the human dimension that, absent a polar opposite, a thing (object, person, characteristic, etc.) never enters your awareness. This is a key takeaway because it means that polarity requires you to experience what you might call "bad" so that you might also experience what you call "good." *Satyagraha*. This insight brings truth to the never-ending question of why our experience of the HD must include such misery as dishonesty, corruption, violence, disease, natural disaster, and so on.

Polarity is your special tool for your awareness and understanding of the HD. It is the mechanism by which all things materialize for you and how you assign meaning to each. Only with polarity do you come to experience and, ultimately, *create* all that is in the HD. There is no exception to this. This is the truth. It is constant and constructive.

Human Geometry 101

How does polarity work? With polarity you experience everything in the human dimension by making a comparison between two distinct *points*, such as two contrasting qualities, distinct objects, opposing positions, etc., and evaluating the difference between them. This happens in the case of all material form (cars, people, furniture, trees, etc.), as well as nonmaterial form (sound, light, odor, taste, feelings, emotions, etc.). *Evaluate* is a befitting term here because it suggests an assessment of *value* for the difference between every set of two points, for example the number of inches between two objects or the different degrees of temperature between two cities. The *value* between each two points also helps to define the *relationship* between them. You experience all people and things in this comparative, or relative, manner.

You have likely heard the human dimension figuratively referred to as our "plane of existence," or "personal space." As it turns out, *dimension, plane,* and *space* are all suitable words to use for understanding polarity because they are common terms used in geometry, the branch of mathematics that focuses on the configuration and relative properties of things. Just as mathematics is considered the language for understanding science, geometry is the language for understanding polarity. For some truth seekers, it is reassuring to learn that there is a mathematical and scientific basis for the application of polarity to the human dimension.

You were probably introduced to geometry in high school, perhaps even earlier. This is because neuroscience has shown us that the human brain's capacity for logical thinking is more highly activated during the middle teenage years. As a mid-teen, you probably didn't realize just how relevant geometry was to your life. Now it is geometry that provides the foundation for understanding just how you work with polarity to create and experience everything in the HD. Welcome to Human Geometry 101!

The basic unit of geometry is the *point.* By definition, a single point represents a specific location in space. It has no mass or dimension. In geometry, a point is represented by a dot, identified with a capital letter, as shown by Points A and B in Figure 1 below.

A geometric *line* is formed when two points are connected. Every line must contain at least two points. A line is one-dimensional, measured only by length, extending into infinity in two opposite directions, as depicted in Figure 1. There is a difference that establishes an "is-is not" relationship between every set of two points on a line. For example, in Figure 1, that which *is* Point A is distinct from, or *is not*, Point B. The *relative* difference between every set of two points establishes a connection or *relationship* between them that can be quantified by assigning a *value* to each point, as well as to the difference between them. For example, if Point A in Figure 1 is assigned the mathematical value of 7, and Point B a value of 2, then the difference, or relationship, between Point A and Point can be quantified, or described, by the value of 5.

Figure 1

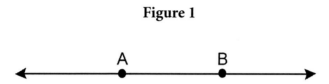

When two lines intersect, they form a geometric *plane.* A plane is two-dimensional, measured by length and width. In geometry, a plane is usually represented by an *x-axis* and *y-axis,* as illustrated in Figure 2 below.

Figure 2

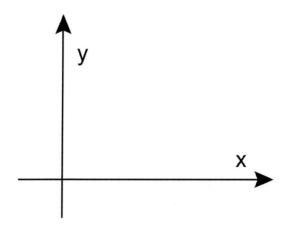

A *space* is made up of an infinite number of planes. It is the sum of all points, lines, and planes. In other words: space is *all that is.* It has no boundaries and extends infinitely in all directions. Space is three-dimensional, measured by length, width, and height. This third dimension of space is represented by adding a *z-axis* to a plane, as shown in Figure 3 below.

Figure 3

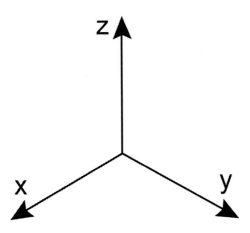

You experience all people and material things in the human dimension spatially, or three-dimensionally. So, you could say that the HD is 3-D, as evidenced by your awareness of the buildings, furniture, books, computers, people, etc. in the space currently surrounding you. In fact, you are so accustomed to a three-dimensional world, that sometimes you even put on those stylish 3-D glasses in the movie theater to experience the action jump off the 2-D movie screen, resembling the 3-D world you know. In geometrical terms, all the people and material things of the HD are *figures*. Figures in space are called *solids* or *surfaces* and are formed by any combination of points, lines, or planes. For example, the figure of a house is formed in the space around you by connecting points, to form lines, which then intersect to form planes. Boom! You have a 3-D house in the HD. Each of these basic components of geometry is shown in Figure 4.

Figure 4

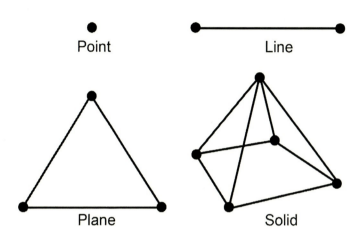

Point   Line

Plane   Solid

Form in the Human Dimension

It only takes a quick lesson in geometry to understand just how essential polarity is to your experience of the human dimension. I use *form* to describe much of what comprises your experience of the HD. There are *solid* or *material* forms (i.e., book, tree, car, people), *gaseous* forms (i.e., oxygen, helium, carbon dioxide), liquid forms (i.e., pools, ponds, oceans), sound forms (i.e., music, talking, birds chirping), *light* forms (i.e., sunlight, candlelight, rainbow), and so on. Once again, forms arise from one or more sets of points, with a value differential between them. For example, *hot* (Point A) and *cold* (Point B) have a temperature value differential, whereas light (Point A) and *dark* (Point B) have a lux value differential. You know that some forms within the HD are more pleasing to you than others. Even your experience of *pleasant* (Point A) versus *unpleasant* (Point B), a common polarity in the HD, has a value differential, although this one is much harder to gauge.

The "U-axis"

There is one more important part to your lesson on Human Geometry 101. This is where *you* come into the picture in a big way, both figuratively and literally. This is where you begin to glimpse the truth of just how amazing you are. Here it is: the relationship between *you* and all other points, lines, planes, and space that make up the HD produces yet another dimensional line—a *fourth dimension*. With *you*, the 3-D axes of *x, y,* and *z* are joined by a fourth axis and, because it is all about *you*, I call this the *you-axis*, or "*u-axis*" for short. With you, the HD is no longer 3-D, but 4-D. The human dimension is the dimension of *you* and all human beings. It is comprised of all the forms arising from the *point*, or *point of view,* that is *you*, as illustrated below. This is the very simple, geometric, and mathematical foundation of the human dimension. These basic geometrical elements provide the structure and framework for the entire HD.

Figure 5

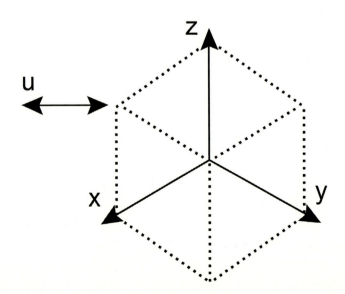

Your individual evaluations of all the relationships between *you* and all other points, lines, planes, and space is what creates your experience of the HD. Polarity is the tool you use to make these evaluations. Following your evaluations, the sum of the choices you make is what ultimately determines the quality of your experience. You make these choices every moment of every day. For example:

- It's too hot to go to the beach today, so I'll go shopping instead.
- I'll drive faster to get there earlier.
- I want the blueberry lavender ice cream.
- My boss has a great sense of humor, so I'm sticking with this job.
- I'm going to redecorate my outdated bedroom.
- I'm voting for the Republican candidate.

These are the types of more obvious evaluations and choices you routinely make to illustrate how *you* and all human beings create and experience the HD together, on both an individual and collective level. It is that simple.

Who are you? You are the creator of your experience. Now the parts of the whole, grand, fully integrated picture begin to come together. As this journey of remembering unfolds, you are in store for more illuminating satyagraha moments. Chapter 7 delves further into exactly how you work with polarity to create all that you experience in the HD, and Chapter 9 adds more layers to the significance of polarity as you explore the relationships created between you and all that surrounds you in the HD.

The Major Polarities of the HD

Your life in the HD is built with, and revolves around, a vast network of polarities. Everywhere you turn, and even when you are still, countless lines of polarity extend between infinite points to shape your experience of the HD. Even if it was possible to identify each and every polarity, your brain would not be able to process the enormity of it all. Thankfully, most of your experience of the HD comes by way of just four major polarities which are applicable to nearly every moment of your life. Understanding these four essential polarities can help you remember who you are, inform the life choices you make, and forever alter your experience of the HD. Here is your introduction to each:

1. Yin and Yang

Yin-yang is the energy, or force of expression, behind all form, both material and non-material, and all phenomena appearing in the human dimension. It is the *mother-father* of all polarities. The traditional schools of Chinese philosophy and science suggest that yin-yang originates from *taiji*—a state of undifferentiated and infinite potential, the oneness of all things before polarity arises, and the absolute source of all human reality. Yin-yang is the instance of taiji in the HD experienced with polarity, that is, differentiated, opposite, interconnected, and balanced sets of two.

The nature of this polarity was first expressed in the third century BCE by philosopher Zou Yan, the founder of Chinese scientific thought. Many of his teachings were later incorporated into Taoism and Confucianism. In Mandarin the word *yin* refers to the cool, shady side of a mountain, whereas *yang* refers to the bright, sunny side. Together yin-yang represent the dual, or *polar*, nature of life in the human dimension, meaning that all experience of the HD arises from contradictory and complementary pairs.

Yin represents the receptive, inward, tranquil, and passive expressions of yin-yang, whereas yang exhibits the projective, outward, restless, and active qualities. The countless examples of yin-yang include form and phenomena such as hard and soft, fire and water, birth and death, male and female, day and night, work and play, conflict and resolve, sleeping and waking, left and right, up and down, and even the inhale and exhale of your breath.

It is important to highlight the paradoxical truth that yin and yang are two different and opposite expressions (polarities) of a single undifferentiated whole. They are interdependent, meaning that, to be complete, the expression of one requires the expression of the other. One always follows the other, without exception, emphasizing the inseparable and dynamic connection between the two. In the human dimension, to have the experience of yin, you must also experience yang. The fundamental Taoist text, *Tao Te Ching*, written by Lao Tzu, describes this phenomenon beautifully:

When the world knows beauty as beauty, ugliness arises

When it knows good as good, evil arises

Thus being and non-being produce each other

Difficult and easy bring about each other

Long and short reveal each other

High and low support each other

Music and voice harmonize each other

Front and back follow each other.[14]

In Western scientific terms, the nature of yin-yang is similarly expressed by Newton's Third Law, which states: "For every action there is an equal and opposite reaction."[15]

Yin and yang signify the everlasting cycle of change, thus, creation in the human dimension. When something is divided into two, such as taiji into yin and yang, the equilibrium of wholeness is upset and

---

14. Derek Lin, n.d. "Tao Te Ching Online Translation." Taoism.net. Accessed February 18, 2023. https://taoism.net/tao-te-ching-online-translation/.
15. "Newton's Laws of Motion." NASA Glenn Research Center. Accessed February 18, 2023. https://www1.grc.nasa.gov/beginners-guide-to-aeronautics/newtons-laws-of-motion/

the two expressions of the whole chase after each other, seeking unity, harmony, and balance. Yin-yang, therefore, is not static. Its nature is to continuously ebb, flow, and change, as depicted by the traditional symbol of yin-yang in Figure 6 below, in which two opposites are conjoined, both having a speck of the other at its core. You can appreciate why yin-yang is truly a fundamental polarity, so much so that all other polarities in the HD are its derivatives.

Figure 6

2. This and That

This polarity is perhaps the most recognizable. Like yin-yang, but not as broad in scope, this polarity pertains specifically to all form (not phenomena) in the human dimension, originating from the formless state of taiji. It is experienced through contrasting polar opposites, beginning with the two fundamentally distinct forms of body (*material form*) and mind (*conscious form*). The examples of this polarity go on *ad infinitum* to include light-dark, high-low, left-right, fast-slow, loud-quiet, smooth-rough, fragrant-stenchy, sweet-savory, etc. and essentially all the polarities that define form in the HD. I refer to this familiar polarity as *this-that*.

This-that is especially relatable since you experience its countless variations with your five senses, continuously, in every second. As you are aware, some varieties of this-that are pleasing to you, whereas others are not, and the degree of pleasant-unpleasant, another polarity in itself, can vary from person to person.

3. Love and Fear

Though much more subtle, *love-fear* is another highly familiar polarity. Love and fear are the two fundamental and distinct human emotions that provide us with an experience of the movement (vibration or pulsation) of the one, absolute, unifying, universal energy within the HD. Just as this-that permits our experience of formlessness in the HD, love-fear allows us to experience of this pervasive energetic motion.

People often consider *hate* to be the opposite of *love*. Hate, however, is just one example of a *feeling* that arises out of fear. Anger and anxiety are two other examples of such feelings. While your experience of life includes a wide range of feelings, all feelings originate from the two emotions of love and fear. There is no exception to this. You know, very well, that these two powerful emotions regularly influence, not just your feelings, but also your everyday choices and actions. Chapter 7 will give you a closer look at the connection between feeling and emotion and how they affect your experience of the HD.

The truth of love-fear is aptly expressed by God's words in the book *Conversations with God—Book 1,* by Neale Donald Walsch:

Fear wraps our bodies in clothing, love allows us to stand naked. Fear clings to and clutches to all that we have, love gives all that we have away. Fear holds close, love holds dear. Fear grasps, love lets go. Fear rankles, love soothes. Fear attacks, love amends.

Every human thought, word, or deed is based in one emotion or the other. You have no choice about this, because there is nothing else from which to choose. But you do have the choice about which of these to select.[16]

Walsch goes on to suggest that the nature of love is to create, include, integrate, collaborate, heal, ease, accept, compromise, embrace, share, reveal, expand, send out, stay, engage, open up, and see possibilities. Love is patient and kind.

Conversely, the nature of fear is to destroy, divide, separate, compete, harm, force, reject, confront, recoil, hoard, hide, contract, draw in, flee, disengage, shut down, and see limitations. Fear is impatient and unkind.

Love-fear shows up often in your everyday life. Think of the times you put people, things, or events into the general buckets of *good* or *bad*. On these occasions, what you are really doing is making a choice somewhere on the line of emotion between the points of love and fear. For example, you might say you are stuck in a "bad" job. But what has really got you stuck is your fear. It could be your fear of change, speaking up to improve a situation, or losing a good income, etc. The job is the job—neither good nor bad—but in this case you are experiencing it through the emotion of fear.

4. Past and Future

If you are like most people, time rules your life. Your feet are firmly planted on a timeline somewhere between the two points of *past* and *future*. This is readily confirmed by observing your thoughts as you go

16. Neale Donald Walsch, *Conversations with God—Book 1* (New York: G. P. Putnam's Sons, 1995), 19.

about the day. As you do, you will see that your mind is usually focused on what you did before (past) and what you will do next (future). Only occasionally, if ever, does your mind come to rest upon what you are doing in the present moment. Interestingly, when it does, your mind becomes still. You are literally *out of your mind* in that moment.

Science has always struggled with the concept of time. Theoretically speaking, linear time is a domain separate from the human dimension. It runs in one direction, from past to future, beginning with the Big Bang more than 13 billion years ago when, hypothetically, the universe began. Although the concept of linear time has never been proven scientifically, it still forms the basis for many of the choices you make in life.

I will cut to the chase and assert that, in truth, linear time is an illusion. I know this is a bold assertion because we are all keenly "tuned in" to past-future. This is because past and future serve as two reference points for our minds to comprehend and evaluate the vast possibilities from which we may experience the present moment. The celebrated spiritual teacher and author of *The Power of Now*, Eckhart Tolle, makes this point beautifully:

On the surface, the present moment is "what happens." Since what happens changes continuously, it seems that every day of your life consists of thousands of moments in which different things happen. Time is seen as the endless succession of moments, some "good," and some "bad." Yet, if you look more closely, that is to say, through your own immediate experience, you find that there are not many moments at all. You discover that there is only ever this moment. Life is always now. Your entire life unfolds in this constant Now. Even past or future moments only exist when you remember or anticipate them, and you do so by thinking about them in the only moment there is: this one.[17]

Tolle underscores the truth about time by inviting you to "focus your attention on the Now, and tell me what problem you have in the moment."

It makes perfect sense that the English word *time* comes from the ancient Proto-Indo European (PIE) word *da*, meaning to *divide* or *cut up* because, although time is an illusion, past-future does serve us in the HD as the odds calculator with which our minds compile, sort out, and organize the various options to choose from in order to experience the HD, each option deriving its meaning by comparing it to all others. This process becomes apparent when you notice how often in the present moment you are apprehensive versus hopeful for the future, or reminiscent versus regretful of the past.

The Truth About Polarity

These four major polarities provide the framework for your experience of the human dimension. In this way they are, indeed, *constructive*, but the structure they provide is not *constant*. You know this simply by looking around you and observing how the human dimension is forever changing. The truth about polarity and the entire HD, therefore, is that they are *not* true. They cannot be true because they are not *both* constant *and* constructive—the two defining qualities of truth. In truth, the HD is an illusion. It is all smoke and mirrors.

This is not a new idea. Eastern religion and philosophy, particularly the Hindu teachings of the *Vedas, Upanishads,* and *Puranas,* called this illusion *maya.* This Sanskrit word originally referred to a god's magical powers that concealed the truth, however, maya is now translated

17. Eckhart Tolle, *A New Earth: Awakening to Your Life's Purpose* (Penguin Life, 2008), 204.

simply as *illusion* or *appearance*. It is maya that enables our temporal experience of the human dimension, and it is in maya's embrace that we forget the truth of *who we are, where we came from,* and *why we are here,* that is, the meaning and purpose of life.

Renowned spiritual leader, Sri Sri Ravi Shankar says this about maya:

Maya means illusion. Maya means that which is temporary, that which is not the truth. Maya simply means appearance. Like the sunset is maya because it only appears to be setting. In reality (truth) it is not setting. So sunset is maya.[18]

Rabindranath Tagore, the first non-European writer to be awarded the Nobel Prize for Literature in 1913, brings in a Western perspective by saying:

Our self (Soul) is maya (an illusion) where it is merely individual and finite, where it considers its separateness as absolute; it is satyam (Truth) where it recognizes its essence in the universal and infinite, in the Supreme Self, in paramatman (God). This is what Christ means when he says, "Before Abraham was, I am" (i.e., before Abraham was God, who is the same that is in my soul—I am That.)[19]

This all means that what you generally call your *reality*, is *not* real at all. Polarity and the entire human dimension exist, temporarily, thanks to the magic of maya. Admittedly, this does sound somewhat like the movie *The Matrix*. But, in truth, what you experience as the human

---

18. "Summary of Bhagavad Gita Chapter 7—Part 3." The Art of Living. Accessed February 19, 2023. https://www.artofliving.org/wisdom/summary-bhagavad-gita-chapter7-part3

19. "Our self (Soul) is maya . . ." AZ Quotes. Accessed February 19, 2023. https://www.azquotes.com/quote/535597

dimension is countless sets of *polar* opposite points, wherein *one* is expressed as *two*.

One undifferentiated *taiji* is expressed as *yin* and *yang*.

One unified *formlessness* is expressed as *this* and *that*.

One universal *emotional* energy is expressed as *love* and *fear*.

One sum of all possibility is expressed as *past* and *future*.

What is *true*—constant and constructive—is the taiji, formlessness, emotional energy, and possibility. The *illusion* is your experience of each of these as the polarities of yin-yang, this-that, love-fear, and past-future.

Do not interpret this in a way that diminishes your experience of the human dimension. Instead, it means that the HD is part of something much bigger and truer. As a truth seeker, you already know this. By its own definition, to experience polarity, you must also have the capacity to experience what polarity is *not*, because with polarity, it is the relationship between two polar opposites that allows you to comprehend both. The truth only exists *relative* to what is untrue. Paradoxically, then, polarity is *both* the device that pulls you into the illusion of the HD and the means to escape the illusion by experiencing what polarity is *not*.

This all leads to some rather obvious and important questions:

What, then, is not polarity?

If the human dimension is not real or true, then what is?

If polarity is the framework of the HD, and it is not true, then where does this framework reside?

Ready for more satyagraha? The answers to these questions take you further down the path of remembering the spectacular truth of *who you are* and *where you came from*—what you might call the *absolute* truth.

Sati Three: Breath Polarities

1. Find your seat (refer to Sati One, if needed) and get settled.
2. Begin with a slow, deep inhale to the count of four, then slowly exhale to another count of four. Repeat this breath five times. In yoga and meditation, the practice of balanced breathing is called by its Sanskrit name: *sama-vritti.*
3. Now, with your eyes still closed, return your breath to its normal rhythm, and spend two minutes observing where in your body you most clearly sense your breath.

    At the rise and fall of your chest?
    With the filling and emptying of your belly?
    In the coolness and warmth in your nostrils or across your upper lip?
    Where else?
4. Then, for the next two minutes, shift your awareness and look for the pairs of *this-that* opposites, which allow you to experience breathing.

    In-out?
    Rise-fall?
    Cool-warm?
    Up-down?
    Desire-fulfillment?
    Distraction-focus?
    Calmness-stress?
    What others?
5. Finally, relax your awareness and open your eyes.

Breathing, like everything you do in the human dimension, is experienced only with the tool of polarity. The life-sustaining act of breathing began the moment you were born in the human dimension and has been your constant companion ever since, just like every other polarity of the HD. Here is a homework assignment: As you go about your day, pause occasionally, and look for other polarities that enable your experience of life in the human dimension. You will discover that they are everywhere, all the time.

④

Absolute

The Great Way isn't difficult
   for those who are unattached to their preferences.
Let go of longing and aversion,
   and everything will be perfectly clear.
When you cling to a hairbreadth of distinction,
   heaven and earth are set apart.
If you want to realize the Truth,
   don't be for or against.
The struggle between good and evil
   is the primal disease of the mind.
Not grasping the deeper meaning,
   you just trouble your mind's serenity.
As vast as infinite space,
   it is perfect and lacks nothing.
But because you select and reject,
   you can't perceive its True nature.
Don't get entangled in the world;
   don't lose yourself in emptiness.
Be at peace in the oneness of things,
   and all errors will disappear by themselves.[20]
—"The Mind of Absolute Trust," by Seng-Ts'an

---

20. "The Mind of Absolute Trust," by Seng-Ts'an. *Poetry Chaikhana: Sacred Poetry from Around the World.* Accessed February 19, 2023. https://www.poetry-chaikhana.com/Poets/S/SengTsan/Mindof/index.html

Imagine, for a moment, being in a place with no light or dark, no up or down, no left or right, and no hot or cold. No quiet or loud—no sound at all. No before, after, beginning, middle, or end. No space. No time. No pleasant or unpleasant. Can your mind conceive of a state without polar opposites? Can you visualize the *Great Way*, as depicted by Seng-Tsan above—an existence that is completely *unified, undivided, and whole?*

Even if you float around in a sensory deprivation tank for a couple hours, it is hard to conceive of such a state because here, in the human dimension, the entirety of your experience unfolds only through pairs of contrasting polar opposites. This phenomenon is not unlike the pairings of "0" and "1" in the character strings of the binary code, which provides the processing instructions for nearly every computer program. Like the binary code, everything you experience in the HD is based on your evaluation of the relative difference between a "true and false," "this and that," or "is and is not." This is the way of polarity in the human dimension. But as you just discovered, polarity, and the human dimension it holds together, are mere illusions.

What is *not* an illusion is an altogether different state of being that is singular, undivided, complete, and whole. It is the domain that encompasses all parts of this integrative "parts to whole" journey to truth. In this alternative plane of existence, the relative "this and that" of polarity does not exist and might even seem just as bizarre as a world without polarity might seem to you. It is what I am calling the *absolute*, and it is from this *absolute* perspective that the simple truth of *it all* originates. After all, what can be more simple than *singular, undivided, complete, and whole?*

Most importantly, however, is that the absolute is *where you came from*. It is your source and origin and the home to you and everything you know and experience. The upcoming chapters offer an opportunity for you to remember exactly how you emerged from the absolute and showed up here in the human dimension. But first, we must lay a foundation with a more complete description of the absolute. Here is where the truth about you really begins.

The Nature of the Absolute

The absolute is a *metaphysical* (*beyond* physical), *metapolar* (*beyond* polarity), *true* (constant and constructive) realm, which precedes, encompasses, and transcends humanity and the human dimension. You can think of the absolute as a state of being, another dimension or plane, an omnipresence, or even a container that holds all that is. And because, here, in the HD, polarity is essential for understanding everything, even the absolute, you might even consider the absolute to be polarity's polar opposite.

It is not easy to describe this absolute state of being with words that were developed for the utterly different human dimension. The English word *absolute* comes from the fourteenth century French word *absolut,* which was intended to express the "condition of not relative to something else." So it seems, then, that *absolute* is a fitting choice to represent the incomparable and all-encompassing nature of this alternative dimension.

The biggest obstacle to articulating the nature of the absolute, however, is the human mind's endless preoccupation with the copious "is-is not" relationships of polarity, whereas, by contrast, the absolute operates on an altogether different schema. Within the absolute, there is no *is not*. There is only a singular *is,* sometimes referred to by truth seekers as the great *isness, singularity,* or as I do here, the *absolute.* Naturally, we want the absolute to be a person, place, or thing, but it is none of the above. Using the words available to us, the precise nature of the absolute is best conveyed by its two defining qualities. That is, the absolute is both:

- perfect, and
- true

Admittedly, to say a thing is "perfect and true" conjures up idealistic images of valiant knights, virgin brides, and trusty Boy Scouts. And while the absolute certainly encompasses these virtuous ideals, its scope is much broader. The absolute is not perfect in the usual sense of "flawless," because it includes what you might consider to be flawed. Instead, it is perfect in the sense of being complete, fulfilled, and utterly evolved.

The absolute is the source and definitive point of origin for you and the entire human dimension. But whereas the human dimension is founded upon the *twos* of polarity, the absolute is based on *oneness*. It is the singular, unified, coalesced *whole*—the fully integrated *all that is* rolled up into one. Just as pure white light is the sum of all colored light, the absolute is the sum of *all that is*, including even the illusion of polarity and the human dimension.

Furthermore, if the sum of *all that is* isn't large enough, the absolute also contains the sum of *all that might be,* in other words, all *possibility* and *potential* available to you in the human dimension. Applying the vocabulary of human geometry from Chapter 3, we could say that the absolute is the sum of all the points of polarity, both known and *unknown,* because the absolute encompasses all form that you experience in the HD and all form that you may *potentially* experience. All opportunity originates from the absolute, such that the absolute contains both the present you and the potential you. Now, you can appreciate just how BIG the absolute truly is.

In its singular, unified, and whole state of being, the absolute embodies everlasting balance and harmony, lacking nothing and seeking nothing more. After all, what more could *all that is* ask for? And because there is nothing to "rock the boat" or "upset the apple cart," the state of the absolute is one of perpetual stillness, calm, tranquility, and peace–attributes we often long for in the HD.

Lastly, the absolute is also *true*, thus it is *constant* and *constructive* as well as the other qualities that epitomized *truth* from Chapter 2: *universal, infinite, eternal, elemental,* and *structural.* You could even say that truth originates from the absolute. Ontologically speaking, the absolute is the actual, factual, "cut to the chase," "no bullshit," objective reality behind the ever-changing illusion of the human dimension.

As you ponder the "perfect and true" nature of the absolute, images of *paradise, heaven,* or *nirvana* might come to mind. These constructs, however, are the inventions of our "big box" religions. They are based on the model of polar opposites, such as Paradise-Gehenna, heaven-hell, and nirvana-suffering, in which each pair requires you to arrive at an understanding of one in relation to the other. The true nature of the absolute, however, is best represented holistically and integratively, by remembering how all its parts, pairs, and polar opposites fit neatly together, beginning with the part that is *you.*

A Paradox: the HD and the Absolute

With polarity as your only guide for sorting out "what is what" in the human dimension, it is natural that you would want to understand how the human dimension relates to the absolute. But when you start down that path, you inevitably run into a stubborn *paradox,* that is, a condition wherein two seemingly opposite ideas co-exist. In this situation, polarity, a reliable tool for understanding the HD, is insufficient for grasping the magnitude of the absolute. This particular entanglement looks like this:

> *If the absolute is true and encompasses all that is, and if all that is includes the HD, then isn't the HD also true, rather than an illusion?*
>
> *How can the absolute be true, and the HD be part of the absolute, if the HD is not true?*

To help resolve this paradox, I will use the analogy of watching a movie at the theater. From the HD perspective, you are *real*, the theater is *real*, and you are *really* watching the movie. However, as you watch the movie, you are transported from the human dimension to a two-dimensional, flat-screen world, or perhaps even a 3-D world with fancy 3-D glasses. You begin to forget about your own HD reality and experience the action by identifying with the characters in the movie. In doing so, you become immersed in the story and much of your experience of the moment comes through the characters, themes, plot, and action of the movie. Your heartbeat races, you laugh, you cry, and ride a rollercoaster of other feelings, as if you were part of the scene.

As you know, the movie is merely an illusion within the HD, produced by light energy projected onto a flat movie screen. Like a movie, the human dimension is also a captivating illusion within the absolute, produced instead with the magic of polarity. The absolute holds all that is, including what is true (constant and constructive), as well as what is untrue (the illusion of polarity and the HD), even though from the absolute perspective no such distinction exists.

Remembering the Absolute

Perhaps words and metaphors fall short of adequately describing the mysterious realm of the absolute. That is okay. Because the most direct path to remembering the truth of the absolute is not through words or metaphors but through the awareness of your own personal connection to the absolute. Yes, it really is all about *you*.

Accomplishing this ought to be easy because, first, the absolute is everywhere, all the time, 24/7/365, so it is readily available to you. And second, because the absolute is where you came from. It is your home, your source, and the starting point of your journey into the human dimension. When you entered this world, you brought with you a fundamental awareness of your connection to the absolute. Even if it is still largely forgotten, remembering the absolute should come quite naturally for you. But here is the tricky part. To break through to the absolute, you must first get past the mesmerizing illusion of the HD. You must temporarily suspend the activity of your mind, which is captivated by the gazillion *is-is not* and *Point A-Point B* relationships of polarity.

That is the purpose of this journey. The goal of this integrative approach to remembering is to transport you from the world of *twos* to the world of *one*. Doing so reveals, not only how you are related to the absolute, but how the basic parts of you fit together and come into alignment within the absolute—like a metaphysical chiropractic adjustment, popping the parts back into optimal working order. Remembering who you are and your inherent connection to the absolute is one of your natural superpowers, an inherent gift, and your legacy in the human dimension. What you gain from making the effort is elegantly foretold by Seng-Ts'an in the opening quotation of this chapter:

> Don't get entangled in the world;
> don't lose yourself in emptiness.
> Be at peace in the oneness of things,
> and all errors will disappear by themselves.[21]

So, exactly what does it mean for all the parts of you to come into alignment? Just how many *parts* do you really have?

This is the truth about you I promised. You are not just the sum of your fingers, toes, arms, legs, head, and torso. You are not even a mere bundle of organs, cells, molecules, and atoms. You are also far more than the coupling of your body and mind. You are so much more than you might have ever imagined. Your true composition—your *constant and constructive* anatomy—is, well, *absolute*, and therefore radically simple.

---

21. "The Mind of Absolute Trust," by Seng-Ts'an. *Poetry Chaikhana: Sacred Poetry from Around the World*. Accessed February 19, 2023. https://www.poetry-chaikhana.com/Poets/S/SengTsan/Mindof/index.html

You show up in the HD in three basic parts: *soul, body,* and *mind.* But before you arrive in the HD, there is *one* very important intermediary step to getting here. To truly appreciate just how these three parts form the magnificent creature that is you, you must first understand the truth about One.

Sati Four: The Space Between Thought

1. Find your seat (refer to Sati One, if needed) and settle in.

2. Begin by taking a single "cleansing breath"—a slow, deep breath, holding it for a second, then releasing it with an audible sigh.

3. Next, gently inhale to the count of three, and slowly exhale to the count of six, so that your exhale is twice as long as your inhale. This type of uneven breathing is known as vishama-vritti. When the exhale is longer, it is a calming breath. When the inhale is longer, it becomes an energizing breath. This technique can be useful in everyday life situations where you desire more calmness or energy.

4. Take nine more vishama-vritti breaths with a three/six count, longer exhale, for a total of ten such breaths. It might take some practice to get into a rhythm. You may also use a four/eight count if that is more comfortable.

5. Return to your breath's normal rhythm and observe how you feel.

   Do you feel calmer?

   Are your thoughts more active or still?

   What other effect did it have on you?

6. Then, with your eyes still closed, return to your breath's natural rhythm and follow its usual inhale and exhale.

7. As you discovered in Sati Two, it is natural for the focus on your breath to be interrupted by thoughts. This is the normal flow of mindfulness meditation.

8. Now, set aside five minutes to explore your breath, but this time specifically look for the space between each of your thoughts, just as you might look for the blue sky between clouds.

How long does each space between your thoughts last?
In the absence of thought, what is there?
Have you noticed this space before?
How does it feel to recognize this space?

9. Finally, relax your awareness and open your eyes.

The absolute is not easy to recognize amid the chaotic human dimension. We are too preoccupied with the *this-that* polarities that make up our experience. But as you have just witnessed, when you make the time and place, you can glimpse the perfect and true in the stillness between your thoughts. If you regularly return to this absolute space in your mindfulness practice, it becomes even more apparent. In time, you will be able to rest in that place longer and find that this short retreat from the human dimension can bolster your sense of well-being.

One

I am the object of all knowledge,
Father of the world, its mother,
Source of all things, of impure and
pure, of holiness and horror.

I am the goal, the root, the witness,
Home and refuge, dearest friend,
creation and annihilation,
everlasting seed and treasure.

I am the radiance of the sun, I
open or withhold the rainclouds,
I am immortality and
death, am being and non-being.

I am the Self, seated
in the heart of every creature,
I am the origin, the middle,
and the end that all must come to.

Let your thoughts flow past you, calmly;
keep me near, at every moment;
trust me with your life, because I
am you, more than you yourself are.[22]
—The Bhagavad Gita

Now for the *big* picture. The *alpha and omega*. It's time for the deep plunge into the truth about you. You may find it odd to discover that it all begins with the truth about *god*.

Wait. *What?*

This might seem like a rather pointless departure. Perhaps it even makes you a little uncomfortable. The "truth about god" does sound a bit lofty. Afterall, throughout human history, we have never really been able to agree on the idea of god. So, you might think it presumptuous of me to speak about god with such certainty and knowing. Or maybe you just do not believe in god, *any* god. Whether you do or not, it might just seem absurd to try and unravel one of life's greatest mysteries—the existence and nature of god—in such a short book, as if it were even possible at all.

This is where you are wrong. It is where we have all been wrong for a very long time. The notion of getting to the truth about god is not as farfetched as it seems. And "unraveling" the truth of god is precisely what we are doing here. Whatever or whomever you now consider to be god, or *your God,* is not as distantly out there, or up there, as you might have thought. God is closer than you have imagined, or perhaps not yet imagined at all. And by *god*, I am referring to the general concept of god,

---

22. "I am Justice: Clear, Impartial." Poet Seers. Accessed February 20, 2023. Trans. by Stephen Mitchell, based on The Bhagavad Gita an interlinear translation by Winthrop Sargeant. https://www.poetseers.org/spiritual-and-devotional-poets/india/bhagavad-gita/i-am-justice/

not to a specific deity like "the one God" of Judaism or Christianity.[23] Here, I mean any *god*. And whether you believe in a god or not, one thing is certain: you entered the human dimension with absolute clarity about the truth of god but, along with the truth about *who you are, where you came from*, and *why you are here*, you forgot.

The good news is that the truth about god lives on within you. It is built into your DNA and is inherently part of your basic human anatomy. It always has been, and always will be, available to you. Now you have the opportunity to remember, once again, the truth about the sacred connection between the absolute, god, and *you*.

Our Awareness of God

Indisputably, all people, everywhere, are born into the human dimension with an innate awareness of god, whether they eventually come to believe in god, or not. I know this is a bold statement, but it is true. If you are a nonbeliever, you have confronted your awareness of god at some point in your life, evaluated it, and rejected it altogether due to its supernatural ambiguity or empirical insufficiency. If you are a believer, however, you have accepted the existence of some god, and contemplated god's nature and relationship to you, including the prospect of an afterlife in which the two of you could potentially reunite.

Your awareness of a god is as natural and instinctive as your breath. This innate awareness is evidenced universally by the belief of most human beings in some type of divine entity that is bigger, better, more intelligent, more powerful, and more loving than most of us believe ourselves to be.

---

23 In modern English, the grammatical rule requires that the word *god* be capitalized only when used as the name of a specific deity, such as the God of Christianity or Judaism. When referring to the mere concept or general idea of god, as we are here, it is not capitalized.

A 2018 study by the Pew Research Center,[24] shows that 90% of American adults surveyed believe in a god, some higher power, or spiritual force, even though one third of this group says they do not necessarily believe in the God of the Bible.[25] Another Pew study of fifteen Western European countries in 2018 revealed that the majority of people (59–91%) also believe in some type of higher power or spiritual force, even if not the God of the Bible.[26] And, around the world, most people say it is necessary to believe in god to be a moral person.[27]

Whether you realize (remember) it or not, the presence of god in the HD permeates your whole being at a cellular and energetic level. But before we examine why that is, it will help to have a little perspective on the twists and turns in our human history that caused you to forget the truth about god in the first place.

Forgetting God: Shamanism to Religion

Long before any formal concept of *god* existed, and prior to the invention of religion, humanity's innate awareness of the divine was evidenced in our earliest ancestors by their profound connection to one another and the natural world they inhabited. This instinctive sense was the gift

24. The Pew Research Center is a "nonpartisan fact tank that informs the public about the issues, attitudes, and trends shaping America and the world."

25. "When Americans Say They Believe in God, What do They Mean?" Pew Research Center. (April 25, 2018). https://www.pewresearch.org/religion/2018/04/25/when-americans-say-they-believe-in-god-what-do-they-mean/

26. "Being Christian in Western Europe." Pew Research Center. (May 28, 2018). https://www.pewresearch.org/religion/2018/05/29/being-christian-in-western-europe/

27. "Worldwide, Many See Belief in God As Essential to Morality." Pew Research Center. (March 13, 2014). https://www.pewresearch.org/global/2014/03/13/worldwide-many-see-belief-in-god-as-essential-to-morality/

of human evolution. For some unknown reason, about 350,000 years ago, during the Middle Paleolithic period, our *Homo sapien* species distinguished itself from other hominids when our physical brains developed new wiring, giving us the capacity for abstract thought, self-reflection, empathy, and creative expression. Indeed, the Latin word, *Homo sapien*, means "wise or discerning human being."

Humanity, and the human dimension, was forever changed by this evolutionary leap forward. These new evolutionary gifts brought us closer together and paved the way for a more organized and communal way of life centered on shared beliefs, self-expression, and caring for one another. Ultimately, it was our new Homo sapien "superpowers" that allowed our species to outlast its closest evolutionary rival, the Neanderthals, who became extinct some 40,000 years ago. With our new abilities, we began to perceive, then celebrate, our connection to something much bigger than our individual selves. I believe this is also the moment in our history when we first began to ask the same questions we are considering at present: *Who am I? Where did I come from? Why am I here?*

These new human cultural behaviors have been studied and well-documented across many cultures throughout our history. The excavations of some of the earliest human burial sites in the regions of Croatia and Israel from over 300,000 years ago revealed what archaeologists call "intentional" burial sites, containing "grave goods" (artwork, personal possessions, etc.) and sometimes even design work made from the natural pigment red ochre. Anthropologists consider these early human burial practices to be indicative of shared beliefs, cultural rituals, mythology, and "magical" thinking, pointing to the awareness of an afterlife, an immortal soul, and some connection to a higher power.

Enter the shamans. The word *shaman* is believed to have come from the East Asian Manchu-Tungus word *saman*, meaning "one who knows," or perhaps even the earlier Sanskrit word *sramana* signifying a holy person. Recognizing that life's weighty questions of personal meaning, soul, spirit, afterlife, and higher powers were still worthy pursuits in a busy new world, our newly formed Middle Paleolithic communities appointed shamans to specialize in these subjects and oversee such matters, just as they did with other specialized tasks important to community survival, like hunting, farming, tool making, cooking, healing, child-rearing, civic leadership, and so on. Shamans were our earliest religious leaders, and *shamanism* was the precursor to what we call *organized religion* today.

Ultimately, I believe it was shamanism that unwittingly led us away from our inherent awareness of *"who I am, where I came from* and *why I'm here,"* as if to say: "You are busy with your new specialized job and providing for your family, so I will provide the answers to these important questions." As shamans fulfilled this specialized role, new systems of organized religion emerged to preserve the idea of god and define god's relationship to humankind. As these religions flourished, we increasingly began to look outward, turning to the experts for the truth of god instead of inward, where we were focused at the dawn of humanity.

Ironically, as our human brains and, later the fabric of our earliest societies, evolved, we gradually forgot the truth about god that we brought with us into this world. Thus, the same *forgetting* described on the individual neuroscientific level in Chapter 1, occurred on a much broader scale, socially, soon after the dawn of humanity.

Among the earliest recorded religious gods, dating back to 4000 BC, were the Sumerian mother goddess, *Inanna*, her consort and god of shepherds, *Dumuzid*, and *Geshtinanna*, goddess of agriculture and vegetation. Similar deities were worshipped by the Egyptians, Hittites, Phoenicians, and Scandinavians.

Fast forward to the present day. Much of what you now believe about god comes from your religious upbringing and spiritual exploration in adulthood. This includes the *dogmata*—tenets, traditions, and rituals—from one or more of the many historical "big box" religions that seek to bring a clearer understanding of god to the human dimension. Did you know that there are actually tens of thousands of human religions, with nearly as many different versions of god? The *World Christian Encyclopedia: A Comparative Survey of Churches and Religions in the Modern World,*[28] suggests that there are nineteen major world religions, subdivided into 270 large religious groups and many thousands of smaller ones, including 34,000 individual Christian groups, each with a slightly different take on the nature of god.

God in Our Language

The field of *linguistics* gives us insight, not only into language, but also the beliefs of its speakers and, in this case, our beliefs about god. The modern English word *god* comes from the Proto-Germanic word *gudan* or *guthan* (*circa* 500 BC), which is further traced back to *ghut* or *ghutam,* a PIE word meaning "to call" or "invoke" (*circa* 3000-4000 BC). *God* is also linguistically related to the Sanskrit word *hu* or *huta,* meaning "one to whom a gift is offered," used as far back as the ancient Hindu scriptures of the *Rig Veda* (circa 1500 BC). Similarly, the Latin language versions of *dio, dios, deus,* and *dieu* have PIE origins meaning "sky or heaven."

Interestingly, the capitalized version of the word *god* is relatively new in history—only about 1,400 years old (circa 600 AD). *God,* capitalized, was never used in any of the manuscripts of ancient Judeo-Christian scriptures written in Hebrew, Aramaic, Greek, or Latin. The

28. David B. Barrett, et. al., *World Christian Encyclopedia: A Comparative Survey of Churches and Religions in the Modern World 2 Volume Set.* (USA: Oxford University Press, Second Edition, 2001).

practice of capitalization is traced to the *Silver Bible*, a 6th century Gothic translation of the four Gospels that was penned in silver ink. It was here that we first gave God her own separate, capitalized name, as if to further distinguish her from you with your individual capitalized name.

There is an equally rich linguistic tradition related to our understanding of *god* in most all languages, as evidenced by the multitude of mystical and religious writings throughout the ages. You already know that there are countless interpretations and versions of the Bible, Qur'an, Bhagavad Gita, Tao Te Ching, Talmud, Book of Mormon, Egyptian Book of the Dead, and so on. This vast library is augmented by the writings of notable philosophers, psychologists, spiritual thinkers, truth seekers, and reformers throughout history, including Plato, Aristotle, Confucius, St. Thomas Aquinas, Descartes, Leibniz, Jung, as well as popular contemporary thought leaders such as the Dalai Lama, Sadhguru, Sri Sri Ravi Shankar, Jamal Badawi, Joel Osteen, Billy Graham, Eckhart Tolle, and Neale Donald Walsch, to name just a few. Given this far-reaching quest for the truth about god, spanning world cultures and eras, one thing seems certain: god is evidently there, somewhere. We are not just making this stuff up.

God *Is*

We have clearly been talking about god for a very long time. Since before the invention of shamanism, to today's organized religions, our collective awareness of a god, or pantheons of gods, has flooded our language with words we use to portray the divine. Our countless ideations of god have been given many names: *El, Yahweh, Elohim, Allah, God, Shiva, Vishnu, Hari, Jehovah, I Am That I Am, Baha, Brahma*, and so on.

Unquestionably, the true significance of all this spiritual and religious thinking and writing about god is that, collectively, it reveals and preserves the truth that god exists and that we have some discernible relationship to god, even if that relationship is that of a non-believer. Throughout human history, it has been the religious establishments, despite their missteps and shortcomings, that have kept the "torch of truth" about god burning brightly. The true big picture, and common denominator, among all human beings and religions is that *god is.*

Absolute(ly) God

That "god is" conveys only half of the truth about god. The other half lies in understanding the true nature of god. Amid the diversity of information and writing available to us about god, you might sensibly conclude that it is difficult, if not impossible, to arrive at an understanding of god intellectually. There is simply too much to read and learn. Moreover, each distinct point of view struggles to define and defend its version of god in contrast to all the others, just as the law of polarity dictates. All this effort has produced scores of theological works but no universally accepted version of god. On the contrary, the inconsistencies and shortcomings of our countless religious views of god have, for many people, made god seem, at best, impossible to know and, at worst, unlikely to exist at all.

The god that all of us struggle to remember through our religion, language, and scholarly pursuits, is fundamentally not hard to understand at all. In truth, we are all staring at the same, simple, one god, merely viewed from the many different perspectives we create with polarity. It might surprise you then, that all things considered, there is actually much agreement about the nature of god among most of the world's religious and spiritual traditions. Most depict god as:

- the origin, source, creator
- omnipotent (all-powerful), omnipresent (all-present), omniscient (all-knowing)
- life force, universal consciousness, *spirit, chi, prana*
- arbiter, judge, *karma*

- manifest goodness, perfection, love, peace, harmony, joy, bliss

The sum of this sacred wisdom from countless, diverse cultures throughout human history tells the truth about god and represents what we might call our collective human *memory* of god. In other words, our historic conversation about god is the act of human beings collectively *remembering* what we already know instinctively. God is all of the above—*the source, omnipotent, life force, arbiter, and manifest goodness.* Indeed, god is *perfect* and *true,* or more particularly, *absolute.* This is the human consensus about god. This, all human beings can remember.

The brilliant truth about god has been whispered to you and every one of us throughout the ages. God is absolute. It has been told in scripture, song, and story. You have seen it in art, entertainment, and human interactions. You have watched the truth of god unfold in nature around you and felt it in the core of your being on special occasions. You need only to pay attention to remember what our earliest ancestors knew, and what you already know now. Your personal memory of god is innate. Your experience of god is your birthright. Within you is your proof that god *is* and god is *absolute.*

What is more, there is a fascinating relationship between god and the absolute which is readily understood using the tool of polarity. *God* is the outward, active, and revealed expression of perfect and true, whereas the *absolute* is the inward, idle, passive, and inert expression of these same qualities. You might say that the absolute is the internal state, or condition, of being perfect and true, and god is the external manifestation of this state. God is the absolute in action, extended, reaching out and expressing itself overtly and dynamically. God is the *yang* to the *yin* of the absolute.

To illustrate this, consider the words "I love you." You can feel love toward another inwardly. You can know love's passion quietly. But if you hide love away, its brilliance is never fulfilled. Only when your love is actively and outwardly expressed in your words and actions does love fulfill its greatest promise. In the immortal words of Oscar Hammerstein's *The Sound of Music*: "A bell's not a bell 'til you ring it. A song's not a song 'til you sing it. Love in your heart wasn't put there to stay. Love isn't love 'til you give it away!"[29] God is perfect and true, expressed actively and outwardly in the human dimension.

God = One

To remember god is to unlock the brilliant truth of *who you are, where you came from,* and *why you are* here in the HD, as well as to reveal the special connection between you and the absolute. But the word *god* is itself, a "hot" word. For most people it carries a heavy bias, evokes strong images and meanings, and stirs various emotions. For example, didn't it rattle you just a little when, above, I wrote the words: "we even gave God *her* own separate, capitalized name, as if to further distinguish her from you with your individual capitalized name?"

To resolve this problem, lessen any predisposition you might have, and reduce any symbolic weight you may have already attached to the word *god*, from this point forward, I will refer to this manifestation of perfect and true simply as *One*. God is *One*. There is a majestic simplicity to *One*. It is comfortably secular and broadly inclusive of many beliefs. Doing this helps you to adopt the shoshin (beginner's mind) approach to getting to the truth about One. *One*, the word, will help foster your understanding of *One*, the absolute.

Understanding One

Now you can start remembering what you knew when you showed up here in the human dimension: One *is*, and the nature of One is *absolute*.

---

29. "Sixteen Going on Seventeen" (Reprise) Lyrics. The Rogers & Hammerstein Organization. Accessed February 19, 2023. https://rodgersandhammerstein. com/song/the-sound-of-music/sixteen-going-on-seventeen-reprise/

At the beginning of this chapter, I told you "One (god) is closer than you might have imagined." That is true. And this is where *you* come into the picture in a very big way. Because the most direct path to understanding the connection between One and the absolute is you. Yes, *you.*

Sati Five: Out of Your Mind

1. Find your seat (refer to Sati One, if needed) and settle in.

2. Begin by taking a well-balanced *sama-vritti* breath. This is a slow, deep inhale to the count of four, then a slow exhale to another count of four so that the inhale and exhale are of equal length. You may try a longer count if it feels more comfortable, like five or six.

3. Take another nine *sama-vritti* breaths for a total of ten and notice how you feel.

4. Return your breath to its normal rhythm and spend about two minutes noticing the various sensations (sights, sounds, touches, tastes, smells) that enter your awareness. Likewise, notice your thoughts as they pass through your mind. Refrain from judging any of these visitors to your awareness. Gently accept them all and notice each as they pass through your mind, like clouds passing through the sky.

5. Then, shift your awareness and use your *shoshin* (beginner's) mind to become curious about your awareness itself.

6. This is a subtle, but distinct, difference in focus that is not necessarily easy to do. Spend about five minutes exploring this idea.

> *While your mind is aware of your thoughts and sensations, what part of you is aware of your mind?*
>
> *Does all awareness happen in your mind?*
>
> *Can you step "around" or "out of" your mind and find a broader awareness of you?*
>
> *How does this "out of mind" state of awareness feel?*
>
> > *New and exhilarating?*
> >
> > *Peaceful and still?*

Bigger, broader, and all-encompassing?
Permanent? Constant? Timeless?
Perfect and true?

7.   Finally, relax your awareness and open your eyes.

Since entering the human dimension, your body and mind have continuously changed. And they always will. But in this exercise, for the first time, you might have noticed a part of you that is the same now as it was when you entered the HD, and that will remain unchanged even after you depart. It is your constant and true companion. Along this path, as you assemble all the parts of the whole truth about you, I invite you to listen to *you* about the source and significance of this subtle part of you.

(6)

You

The Truth is inseparable from who you are. Yes, you are the Truth. If you look for it elsewhere, you will be deceived every time.[30]
—Eckhart Tolle, *A New Earth*

FINALLY, WE GET TO *YOU*.

Now we take an enlightening look at *you* and the parts of you that make up your *true* human anatomy: *soul, body,* and *mind.* As you become familiar with each of these parts, you are afforded an ideal opportunity to rediscover your special connection to One and the absolute, moving you closer to the whole truth about *who you are, where you came from,* and *why you are here.* Get ready. You are about to see just how magnificent you really are.

At this point you might be thinking: "This is a heck of a lot to take in." Maybe you can embrace the concept of polarity and the idea that you exist in a human dimension. Perhaps, even, the notion of an absolute seems perfectly reasonable. But it might be a step too far to replace your comfortable word *god,* with the new and unconventional word, *One.*

This is provocative stuff. I remind you that an encounter with satyagraha—truth force—is not always easy. Remembering is a process. It is, in many ways, a journey back to where you came from, filled with incredible twists, turns, and transformative surprises. Truth seeker, take

30. Eckhart Tolle, *A New Earth: Awakening to Your Life's Purpose,* (Penguin Life, 2008), 71.

a moment here to reset your beginner's mind and let this integrative "parts to whole" course reveal the entirety of the truth about you.

The Truth About You

With *you* it all comes together. The reason for this is very simple, and also deeply inspiring. Here it is:

Just as One is the outward and active expression of a perfect and true absolute, so, too, are you the expression of a perfect and true One in the human dimension.

You are the manifestation, the revelation, of One—perfect and true—in the human dimension.

You are One.

In truth, we are all One.

That is a lot to take in. If it is hard to accept this truth at first, it is probably because throughout your life you have been told, both directly and implicitly, that you are "less than" and "separate" from One. This has been your programming—the programming of polarity—the "is-is not," "true-false," and "us-them" pairs of the HD. It goes something like this: you can know One only in relation to that which One is not, and One is most certainly *not* you. You, human, are the polar opposite of One. *Ouch!*

You have been misled.

Fortunately, now you can remember the truth of it all. One is the active expression of the absolute, and you are the phenomenon, the appearance, the presence of One in the human dimension. Now you have the words and a new framework with which to remember this amazing truth about you. This is the forgotten truth that you have known all along. This is "the truth that will set you free."

Five Steps of Human Creation

Let's jump into the details of how you came to be in the human dimension. You already know about *procreation*—the biological process by which your body comes into being. *Procreation* and *creation*, however, are two different things. Procreation is one of many biological processes of the human body, like digestion, metabolism, and breathing. *Creation,* on the other hand, is the act or process of bringing something into being in the first instance. Your creation began well before your body was ever conceived. You could say that, at first, you were a "twinkle in the eye of One." That twinkle was your *soul.* Your journey into this world began with the creation of your soul.

Your soul is the direct expression of One. Just like your body extends and differentiates as an arm or a leg, so does One extend and differentiate to express the qualities of perfect and true as a soul—*your* soul. You know that your body is not your arm *only*, but your arm is *always* part of your body. Similarly, One is not your soul *only*, but your soul is *always* part of One.

After the creation of your soul, things get a little more complicated. In the next step of human creation, your soul extends and differentiates even further to express itself in the human dimension in two parts: body (material) and mind (consciousness). If it helps, you can think of your soul as the *offspring* of One, and your body and mind as the *offspring* of your soul. This is where the biological process of procreation begins. The formation of body and mind by the soul happens at human conception and is realized through the process of gestation and birth. The moment of your birth is the final entry point of One into the HD as a complete, new human being, formed of a soul, body, and mind—in other words, *you.*

You are One, miraculously appearing in the HD as a trinity of *soul-body-mind.* In this way, One may experience Oneself from within the parameters of polarity, not unlike how you might experience yourself while immersed in a book, movie, television show, or video game.

What ultimately unfolds here is that One enters the human dimension in a phenomenal five-step process, with each step forming an essential polarity of human creation. How else could One appear in the HD except by way of polarity? With each successive step, One moves closer to revealing the absolute qualities of perfect and true in the HD, through you. You have just been introduced to the first two steps of the Five Steps of Human Creation. Now take a look at all five steps in Figure 7, below. This is the roadmap for where we are going and what this process looks like.

Figure 7
The Five Steps of Human Creation

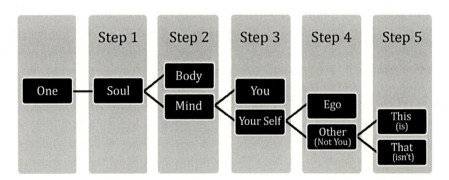

An Energy Hologram

Before we get too far down the road, we need to take a quick detour to make an important point. As the expression of One in the HD, you are formed of the same "stuff" as One. So, what is the "stuff" that you and One are both made of? If you were to reduce you to your smallest, most microscopic and subatomic particles, you would find that, just like One, you are a brilliant collection of distinctive *energies*, each vibrating at different speeds, or *frequencies*. Interestingly, the original meaning of the word *energy* has sixteenth century French roots suggesting "a forceful expression." It is traced further to the Greek word for "activity" or "action." And that is exactly what you are: the forceful expression, or action, of the absolute, as One.

Each of the three parts of you—*soul, body, mind*—vibrates at a unique frequency. Collectively, they produce a three-part energetic *hologram*[31] that is *you*. While it might seem completely reasonable that One is formed of pure energy, the radical notion that you are a human "light bulb" might be harder to accept. This is probably because throughout your life you have been taught that you are a material being—a body—made up of physical matter, with no connection to One, since One is not the subject of science. This lifelong programming has largely contributed your forgetting the truth about the wondrous connection between you and One.

To further complicate matters, it is not necessarily easy to discern the energies of soul, body, and mind within you, especially if you are not aware that they exist in the first place. But they do exist. Their hologram, that is to say, *you*, are a cohesive symphony of energy that is awesome to behold. But just as it can be hard for the untrained ear to distinguish the sound of different instruments in an orchestra, it is equally difficult to sort out the three primary energies that compose the masterpiece of you.

You might have had some inkling of the truth about your energetic composition, even if you did not fully trust it. This truth has been whispered throughout the HD for centuries in our arts and sciences. One example is the great American poet Walt Whitman, who wrote about the energy of the human body in his poem "I Sing the Body

---

31. A hologram is a three-dimensional image formed by a coherent source of light energy.

Electric," composed well before the words "electric" and "electricity" were widely used.

> I sing the body electric,
> The armies of those I love engirth me and I engirth them,
> They will not let me off till I go with them, respond to them,
> And discorrupt them, and charge them full with the charge of the soul.
> Was it doubted that those who corrupt their own bodies conceal themselves?
> And if those who defile the living are as bad as they who defile the dead?
> And if the body does not do fully as much as the soul?
> And if the body were not the soul, what is the soul?
>
> …
>
> O I say these are not the parts and poems of the body only, but of the soul,
> O I say now these are the soul![32]

We will take a closer look at human energy when we discuss the part of you that is your body.

A New Human Anatomy

If you have ever studied anatomy, you probably learned that the human anatomy is comprised of the parts of your body—your head, limbs, torso, organs, systems, and so on. And while this *is* the anatomy of your body, you are not *just* your body. Your true—constant and constructive—anatomy also includes your soul and your mind. Each of these three parts of you—soul, body, and mind—plays an important

---

32. Walt Whitman, "I Sing the Body Electric." Poetry Foundation. Accessed February 19, 2023. https://www.poetryfoundation.org/poems/45472/i-sing-the-body-electric

role in your becoming a uniquely special human being. Let's look at how they come together in the five-step process of your creation. You might be surprised to discover that you are not so different than a human light bulb after all.

Soul

Your soul is where you began. It is the core of your being and the essence of who you are. As a direct expression of One, your soul is the part of you that holds the truth of *who you are, where you came from,* and *why you are here.* Through your soul, you are never *apart* from, but always *a part* of, One. And through your soul, all that is One is equally available to you.

Just like One, your soul is absolute, that is, perfect and true. So, as you might expect, the absolute energy of your soul vibrates at a higher and quicker frequency than the frequencies of your body and mind. The high frequency absolute vibration of your soul energy enables you, sometimes even compels you, to experience your sacred connection to One. When this happens, you become keenly aware of what is true—constant and constructive—and are offered a glimpse into all the possibilities of the absolute. Perhaps you have had such an experience in your life during a nature walk or while meditating. The Sati Practices at the end of each chapter of this book are designed to be a portal to this experience.

Soul: The Original Polarity

With the creation of a soul, One takes the first step toward entering the human dimension as a human being. The formation of your soul is the first and original polarity of your being in the HD. From here countless polarities unfold; first, completing the creation of you, then, the human dimension that surrounds you. The formation of your soul propels the expressive, expansive, and creative energy of One into the

HD through you. As an energetic hologram of soul-body-mind, you personify and emanate this same creative energy and, with polarity as your tool, create all that surrounds you in the HD. You do this with yet another creative process that I call *The Creation Cycle*, which is explained in the next chapter.

As you now know, polarity requires an "is-is not" relationship, or a Point A and Point B, in order to work. But if One is absolute, meaning perfect and true, how is this possible? How can Point A and Point B exist in the realm of the *whole, undivided,* and *complete*? Astonishingly, it is your soul that makes it possible. Your soul is at the center of the mystical paradox that you are *both* part of One and, at the same time, separate from One. To understand this paradoxical truth, I first need to explain the concept of a *self*.

You, Your Self, and One

You might typically think of your *self,* as the same as *you.* But you and your self are quite different. A *self* emerges when an individual becomes aware of its own existence. In other words, your self is you becoming aware of you. This can only happen with some means of reflection that allows you to observe you, as if looking in a mirror. In the human dimension this, of course, involves the two-point system of polarity. A *Point A* must have a *Point B* with which to look back upon and observe Point A. The interaction between Point A and Point B is *relative,* meaning that it establishes a *relationship* between the observer and the observed. This relationship is the self. Your self, then, is not you at all, but the product of you relating to you. The distinction is subtle, but very important.

Your self emerges in the part of you that is your mind in Step 3 of the process of your creation. With your mind you *mentally* reflect upon you, to observe, interact with, and relate to you by thinking. Your self is your mind's awareness and understanding of you, such that your mind serves as your mirror. Accordingly, with the creation of your self in your mind, you become both the observer of you as well as the observed. Do not forget, though, that your self is *not* you but merely the reflection or interpretation of you in your mind. What you truly are is the hologram of soul-body-mind energy.

Created in the Image of One

Now we return to the paradox of the human dimension and the absolute. If One is truly perfect—that is, whole, undivided, singular, and complete—how is it possible for One to have a self which, by definition, requires a separate Point A and Point B? In other words, how does One become two?

The key to unraveling this paradox is first understanding that it is the nature of One to create. After all, One is the active, expansive, and therefore the creative expression of the absolute. One's self is created when One (as Point A) decelerates its absolute energetic frequency in order to differentiate, extend, and form a distinct soul (as Point B). The soul, then, still connected to One, is in a position to reflect its inherent absolute qualities back to One from the perspective of the HD. It is the soul that serves as the mirror for One to experience One's self (or *Oneself*). Your soul is the mirror of the absolute—perfect and true—in the HD.

The process of soul creation highlights the truth that, not only do you and One share the same energetic composition, but you also share the trait of being both the *observer* and the *observed*—you through your self (your mind) and One through One's self (your soul). In both these ways, you are created in the image of One. Or, as it has been whispered many times, in many ways, throughout the ages—you are (all) the children of god.

Body

Most human beings strongly identify with their body. But contrary to popular belief, you are *not* your body. At least, not your body *only*. Your body is just one part of your true, three-part anatomy. The body is formed with polarity, along with the mind, at Step 2 in the creation of every human being. It is one half of the soul's expression as two, *material* (body) and the *conscious* (mind), although from the absolute perspective there is no real distinction.

Your body is the instrument you use to interact and relate with all the other bodies and forms of the HD that you encounter with your five senses: sight, hearing, touch, taste, and smell. In this way your body is both a *receiver* for your experience and a *tool* for your creative expression within the HD. Just like your hand both experiences and creates for you in the HD, so does your body experience and create for One. In truth, your body is the hand of One in the HD.

Body Electric & Eastern Science

To say that your body is *formed* is an accurate description of the process, since your body is one example of many types of *form* in the HD; form being everything that you experience. (See "Form in the HD" in Chapter 3.) Like the formation of the soul, the formation of the body is an energetic process. In order to form a human body and enter the human dimension, soul energy further decelerates to a slower, denser frequency. The frequency of the body's energy is so slow that it takes on a material form. This process is seen in HD as the biological process of conception.

As foretold in Walt Whitman's poem "I Sing the Body Electric," you might already be aware of the energetic nature of the human body and its connection to the soul. Both Eastern and Western sages and scholars have long accepted the truth of an energy field emanating from the human body and have given it many names: chi, prana, life force, spirit, elan, etc.

In Eastern traditions the science of the human body's energy is known as *neigong*. Neigong focuses on chi ("life force" or "life energy"), which is the basis of many Chinese medical therapies, meditation practices, and martial arts, including tai chi. Tai chi uses specified forms of slow movement, coupled with Taoist meditation, to explore the nature of polarity and yin-yang flow in the HD. The goal of this moving meditation is *wu chi*—awareness of the oneness of all things. Through its meditative movement, tai chi offers you the experience of your body's chi (energy), permitting you to work with this energy in a very subtle manner. Practitioners of tai chi attest to the benefits of greater energy and well-being. This may explain why there are an estimated 200 million tai chi practitioners in the world today.

It is important to remember that your body is the direct expression of your soul. Just as the arm of your body extends and differentiates to manifest a hand, so does your soul extend and differentiate to manifest a body. So, when you experience a bodily illness or disease, it is often the result of a damaged or forgotten link between body and soul. This view has been embraced by Eastern science for thousands of years, through holistic-centered soul-body-mind healing practices such as acupuncture, herbal medicine, chiropractic, massage, naturopathy, *shinrin-yoku* (forest-bathing), and so on. Thankfully, these approaches are becoming more accepted among the healing traditions of the West.

The Quantum Truth

It might be easy to accept the idea that your soul is made up of *metaphysical* energy, but it may be harder to embrace the idea that your body is similarly comprised of energy—*material* energy. Material energy is energy of such a slow vibration that it appears in the human dimension as physical matter, that is to say, as solid matter. In truth, your body is human, but it is not solid matter. Your body, and everything you experience as material in the HD, are forms of vibrating energy, appearing within a common, slow, and dense frequency range. Yes, *everything* you experience. This concept requires a significant shift in thinking, especially for those of us in the West. The field of *quantum physics* is credited for helping to bring this truth to the forefront.

Science has shown that all the chemical elements that make up your body, such as carbon, oxygen, hydrogen, etc., are formed by specific combinations of atoms that give each element its unique atomic structure. Those atoms, in turn, are made up of subatomic particles known as protons, neutrons, and electrons, as illustrated in Figure 8.

Figure 8

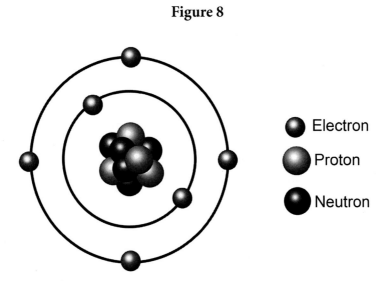

The predominant scientific view has been that these tiny subatomic particles provide the structure for the body and are evidence that the universe is composed of solid material that behaves predictably, according to the laws of physics. What has mattered, scientifically, is solid *matter*.

But in recent years, scientists have observed and concluded that the tiniest particles of an atom behave most often like *waves of energy* rather than like solid matter. Repeatedly, experiments have shown that the behavior of these energy waves is often unpredictable and is, remarkably, influenced by the perception and thoughts of the observer. Although incredible, this means that what you experience as solid matter is, in truth, waves of energy that shift and change according to your thoughts and perceptions. You accomplish this with what I call the *u-axis* of human geometry, introduced in Chapter 3. In other words, you shape your reality. You determine your experience of the human dimension in a process introduced in the next chapter as *The Creation Cycle*. Can you begin to see the parts of the whole truth come together? It really is *all about you*.

Whereas human sensory awareness was traditionally thought to be one way, that is, you observing matter, quantum physics has now established that it is a *two-way* experience. There is always an interaction—an energy *transaction*—between the observer and the observed. The study of these energy transactions, and their link to human energy, are the new scientific frontier in the search for truth. Ironically, it is our *physical* scientists who are leading us to the *metaphysical* truth about life in the human dimension.

An Elemental HD Stew

To be fair, before the rise of quantum physics, traditional science did not entirely forsake us in the quest for the answers to the *who, where,* and *why* questions of this book. Science is credited for developing the periodic table of chemical elements which, to date, identifies 114 chemical elements in the universe.

This is important because it is these chemical elements that constitute all the molecules, that build all the cells, that make up all the organs, that comprise all the bodies and forms of the HD, including not only human forms but also animal, plant, mineral, liquid, and gas forms. Remarkably, your body and all other forms of the HD are largely composed of only six of these 114 chemical elements: hydrogen, oxygen, carbon, nitrogen, phosphorus, and sulfur. These six chemical elements are the primary building blocks, or *ingredients,* of the entire human dimension, making the composition of the HD much simpler than we might have originally thought.

Although you experience these six elements as solid material in all the bodies and forms of the HD, you now know the truth that each of these elements, as well as the other 108, are energy, each vibrating at its own distinct sub-frequency within the broader energy framework of the HD. Within this framework, all bodies and forms (including yours) share these six chemical elements, as if we are all simmering in the same pot of HD stew concocted with a recipe of hydrogen, oxygen, carbon, nitrogen, phosphorus, and sulfur. At the tiniest, molecular level, these ingredients touch, collide, engage, repel, and interact in what was earlier described as energy *transactions,* collectively forming everything we experience in the HD. What's more, this earthly energetic brew is just a small sample of the infinite and eternal energy of the absolute.

Mind

Your mind is the third part of the soul-body-mind hologram of which you are comprised. The mind is formed along with your body at Step 2 of your creation and, like your body, it is part of the expression of your soul as two: *material* (body) and *conscious* (mind). As with the body, the formation of the mind is an energetic process. In this step, the energy of the soul again decelerates to a slower, denser frequency to form a human mind. The frequency of mind energy is not as slow or dense as body energy, which explains why it does not appear as solid matter in the HD, although it is still much slower than that of its parent, the soul.

You are already aware of the energy of your mind. In fact, this energy is seen in your body as brain wave activity since your brain is one of the more obvious locations where your mind and body interact. Your mind, however, is *not* your brain. Your brain is an organ of your body, comprised of material energy, whereas your mind is made of conscious energy. And although, presently, you may believe that your mind engages with your body through your brain *only*, in truth, it also interacts directly with other organs of your body (lungs, stomach, heart, and so on) at the microcellular level without going through your brain. This is especially evident in cases of near-death medical patients who, after declared "brain-dead," upon recovery, can still recall coherent and meaningful events that occurred, suggesting that even when your brain stops working, the mind (consciousness) perseveres.

Unpacking You in the HD

Your mind plays a very special role in the creation of you, your self, and ultimately, the entire human dimension. In Step 3 of your creation, just as One forms a self (*Oneself*) as your soul, your self (*yourself*) is formed in your mind. Here your mind becomes the mirror with which you reflect upon and attempt to understand you in such a way that you become both the *observer* of you and the *observed*. This new self-awareness is also the beginning of *thinking*, as you come to terms with you. Without your thinking mind, you would not be aware of your own existence. This point is neatly conveyed by the French philosopher, Rene Descartes, in his famous words: "Cogito ergo sum" (I think, therefore I am)

After successfully establishing an identity for yourself in the HD, in Step 4 of your creation your mind turns its attention toward all the fascinating other stuff in the HD. As children of the soul, mind, and body are like most children—eager to explore the world. This innocent exuberance sometimes leads them astray from the soul. When this happens, busy mind and body are inclined to forget their soulful origins and give into the pleasures and perils of the human dimension, forgetting who they truly are.

In the mind's enthusiastic exploration, it begins to experience for the first time an "other," or a "not you." This event is marked by the birth of the *ego*—the "me first," and establishes the next polarity in the process of coming into being—the *ego* and the *other*. Newly quipped with a forceful human ego, your mind begins to see yourself as being apart from (instead of a part of) the ubiquitous absolute of your origin, distinct from all that surrounds you in the HD and, most notably, separate from One.

The designation of "other" (or *another*), as used here, refers to all other bodies and forms in the HD, but especially other human beings with very active egos of their own. With the rise of the human ego, we begin to *compete* instead of *collaborate*. We are not competitive by nature, because our nature is absolute so, in truth, there is nothing and no one to compete against. But the ego is competitive by design. Its own survival is predicated on its separation from, and triumph over, all other egos. But remember that you are *not* your ego! Your ego is merely an expression of the self in the HD, created by polarity, masking the truth that you are One.

In Step 5, the final step of human creation, you begin to experience all the *other*, or what is *not* yourself, with the two's of polarity: *this-that* or *is-isn't*. This means that all *other* in the HD—human, animal, plant, mineral, liquid, gas, etc.—only enters your awareness and is understood in terms of its contrasting qualities: hot-cold, dark-light, rough-smooth, bitter-sweet, small-large, etc. Such is the way of polarity.

These five steps culminate in the creation of you, and of every human being in the HD. It is all accomplished with the creative energy—the forceful expression—of One. During this process, the singular truth of you shatters into numerous pieces, allowing you to participate in the illusion of the human dimension. It is these pieces we are reassembling along this journey, so that you can remember the absolute truth about you. You are One.

With your new identity firmly established in the human dimension, you jump into the driver's seat and are off to the races to create your experience of the HD. From this point on, it is all *you*. Just as it is the nature of One to create, so it is your human nature. As is One, so are you. And because you are One, you are a natural creative genius, using polarity as your artistic medium. After all, it is only through a series of polarities that you came to be in the HD in the first place. Your inherent drive to create is unleashed in the HD as you begin to manufacture everything that you experience, along with every other human being. The next chapter is devoted to that very process.

A Divine Gift

While your mind often seems like a mischievous child, it is also an exceptional gift in several important ways. First, it is your mind that makes it possible for you to look upon you and experience you in the HD as a unique self. As pointed out earlier, without your mind, you would have no way of knowing that you exist.

Next, your mind is astonishingly versatile. Formed with polarity, the mind has the *dual* propensity to both *forget* and *remember* the truth about you. In this way, it can be said that you are both *narrow-minded* and *broad-minded*. *Narrow-minded* in the sense that your mind usually focuses *narrowly* on the minutia and countless distractions of the HD. With its domineering ego, the mind is eager to participate in the illusion of being free of any connection to One. On the other hand, you are *broad-minded* in that your mind is equally capable of expansive thought and the intellectual understanding that all human beings are intrinsically connected and unified as One. At a subliminal level, the mind remembers its own origins and "gets" that all minds and bodies are equal expressions of One. In other words, your mind plays a critical role in the process of remembering who you truly are.

Your remarkable human mind is both the curtain that hides the truth and, simultaneously, the opening through which you may glimpse it. This portal between illusion and truth is the basis for many of the so-called mysteries of life. It leads to the joy of discovery and remembering, as well as the anguish of confusion and forgetting because, as you know, it is the nature of polarity that you must know both to experience each. The function of *forgetting* is the nature and purpose of the mind in the human dimension. Since the only way for you to experience something is in relation to that which it is not, you must first forget that you are One, in order to remember the beautiful truth that you have always been One all along. This is the greatest mystery and ultimate paradox of life.

Life and Death

Life and death are another great mystery of the human dimension, and a heavy polarity to contend with. You have already solved half of this mystery by remembering how you enter the human dimension with the Five Steps of Human Creation. But in the HD everything is understood in pairs. In this case, life is paired with death. In the HD, death is ordinarily defined in mechanical terms as the moment when the organs of the body, especially the heart, brain, and lungs, stop functioning. By remembering who you are and how you came to be in the HD, you might now recognize that what happens at death transcends the body, since the body is just one part of you. It is your soul that is the true foundation of your being. And your soul is absolutely eternal.

Death is human creation in reverse. When you die, your humble exit from the illusion of the human dimension is as simple as your modest entrance. As you near death, One begins to withdraw. Rather than extending outward into the HD, the energies of body and mind retract back toward the soul, which then reunites with One and, ultimately, rejoins the infinite and eternal absolute. Of course, while your two feet are still planted in the HD, you experience this process as occurring over time with the *past-future* polarity. In this process, all the polarities of the Five Steps of Human Creation, which brought about your existence in the HD, come to an end, and the entirety of you is reclaimed by the absolute. This is the end of your experience of "this and that" and a return to your experience of perfect and true. It is here that your conscious mind scatters throughout the absolute, and you cease to exist as yourself. You might even say that you "die and go to heaven." Death is, therefore, not an ending, merely a reformation of the wonderful, energetic hologram that is you in the human dimension.

There you have it—the story of you. This is the revelation of your true, three-part human anatomy—soul, body, and mind—and how each of these energetic parts coalesce to form a uniquely beautiful *you*. Now you can remember that your life unfolds from the absolute through a creative five-step process, and at death, you return to the realm of perfect and true from where you came. You are something special, *some-One* more magnificent than you probably ever imagined. This is the amazing truth of *who* you are and *where* you come from.

Now it is time to turn your attention to what you are really up to here in the crazy, mixed-up world of the human dimension. Why are you here? What is your purpose in life?

Sati Six: Body Electric

1. Find your seat (refer to Sati One, if needed) and settle in. Alternatively, for this sati practice, you may lie down on your back in a comfortable position.

2. Begin by taking a cleansing breath: a slow, deep inhale, hold it for a second, then exhale with a gentle, but audible, sigh.

3. Repeat this cleansing breath another two times, then return to your breath's normal rhythm. Notice how you feel after that short breath exercise.

4. Set your watch or timer for eight minutes.

5. With your eyes closed, start by turning your awareness to any sensation which you may feel in your hands.

   Do you feel tingling, pulsing, throbbing, vibration, warmth, cold, stillness, or movement?

6. Then, shift your awareness and slowly scan the individual parts of your body, moving from your hands, to your arms, shoulders, neck, face, torso, abdomen, legs, and feet, resting on each distinct part for a few seconds. Notice the sensations you feel in each. It doesn't matter what order you follow.

   In which body parts do you feel the greatest sensation?
   What does each feel like: pulsing, throbbing, vibration, warmth, cold, stillness, or movement?
   Are any of the sensations sounds, odors, or tastes?

7. At the end of eight minutes, relax your awareness and open your eyes.

During this exercise, it is likely you experienced some subtle, but palpable, sensations in several parts of your body. Each was an opportunity to witness the energy that makes up your body, sometimes called chi, prana, life force, elan, or the "body electric." While this energy is generally seen as being material form, it is part of the energetic "body" of One, to which you are intimately connected via your soul.

Interlude

Three things cannot hide for long: the Moon, the Sun, and the Truth.
—Gautama Buddha

FIVE STEPS AND—*BOOM*—YOU SHOW UP HERE IN THE HD. NOW YOU know the truth of *who* you are and *where you came* from. Before we get to *why you are here*, this is a good place to pause, catch your breath, and review just how far you have come on your journey of remembering. Here is a brief summary of the main ideas you have encountered up to now. These are the initial *parts* of the *whole* truth, which is unfolding before you as you move from chapter to chapter.

- You arrived in this world fully aware of the truth about you: who you are, where you came from, and why you are here.
- While growing up, amid all the distractions of your sensational, new life, you forgot this truth.
- Remembering this truth allows you to realize, once again, what is important and true and rediscover the meaning and purpose to your life.
- Remembering is the process of recognizing a vital, but forgotten, truth, arising from a renewed awareness of how its integral parts relate to the whole.
- Remembering is, therefore, an integrative or "parts-to-whole" approach to getting to the truth.
- For something to be true, it must be both constant and constructive. These are the defining qualities of truth.

- Truth is compelling on its own, and satyagraha—truth force— helps reveal how the true parts of you—soul, body, and mind— integrate and work together.

- The human dimension (or "HD") is the home to all your experience, and polarity is your tool for experiencing your life in the HD.

- With polarity, a thing may enter your awareness only in the presence of its opposite; and a thing is understood only by comparing it to that which it is not.

- In the human geometry of the HD, the u-axis represents the relationship line between you and all other points, lines, planes, and space that make up the geometrical HD.

- The HD and polarity are not true because they are not both constant and constructive.

- What is true is the absolute, defined by the qualities of perfect and true.

- The absolute holds all that is and all that might be, in other words, all the possibility and potential available to you in the human dimension.

- One is the outward, active, and revealed expression of the absolute, and as such, the nature of One is also perfect and true.

- One enters the HD as you, using polarity, in the Five Steps of Human Creation.

- You show up as One in the HD as the sum of three parts: soul, body, and mind, and these parts form your true human anatomy.

- The most direct path to remembering the whole truth of it all is by remembering who you are.

- Your soul is the direct expression of One within you, and through your soul, you are always a part of, and never apart from, One.
- Body and mind are the physical and conscious expressions—the offspring—of soul, and so they are also expressions of One.
- Each part of you—soul, body, and mind—is a unique vibration of energy, and you are the hologram of these three energies vibrating in the HD—a human light bulb!
- These energies originate with the absolute and are revealed by One as you in the HD and, as such, you are the energy (light!) of One in the human dimension.
- Once you show up in the HD, you begin to create everything that surrounds you.
- You are One creating the HD.

Do these ideas seem reasonable and cohesive?

Could this book really be pointing toward something meaningful and important?

These are the right questions to be asking yourself since the process of remembering focuses on listening to *you*.

Or instead, do you find yourself asking:

What are this author's sources?

Where is the evidence for all this?

If this sounds more like you, then remind yourself that the purpose of this journey is to empower you to remember what you already know. You do not *need* a source or evidence. *You* are the source and the evidence.

Think of it this way: When you learned how to ride a bicycle, at first you probably relied on training wheels for support and encouragement to get you going. But at some point, your self-confidence grew, you began to trust yourself, and you let go to experience the exhilaration and joy of riding a bike. It was all you. You mastered the truth of riding a bicycle. Here you are again, on a much bigger bicycle, and on a far more important ride. What will you do?

You can continue to pore over volumes of confusing and conflicting scientific, religious, and philosophical research and writing for validation, or you can listen to you. Despite everything you have been told by the present-day shamans and so-called "experts," it truly is *all about you.* You are, quite literally, the validation and the expert. The force of truth—satyagraha—is asking you to accept responsibility for *who you are.* You are One. I'm here only to remind you of that.

I can appreciate that accepting a new, integrative, "parts to whole" approach to the truth, coupled with trusting yourself on this important subject, is a big ask—even with the help of the *truth force.* It is a lot like assembling a huge puzzle with countless pieces in unusual shapes and colorful patterns, but with the handicap of not really knowing what the final puzzle picture looks like. Even so, when enough pieces come together, you begin to see the whole, big picture. Then, all the confusing parts of the whole puzzle make perfect sense on their own. That is exactly what we are doing here.

$$\left(7\right)$$

Creation

Every living being is an engine geared to the wheelwork of the universe.
Though seemingly affected only by its immediate surrounding,
the sphere of external influence extends to infinite distance.[33]
—Nikola Tesla

YOU ARE AN INCREDIBLE HUMAN BEING. IT IS FAR EASIER TO EMBRACE the wondrous truth about you when you remember exactly how you were formed with the energy of One, that is, the outward and creative expression of the absolute. You are, quite literally, the embodiment of perfect and true. This means you are more worthy, more powerful, more brilliant and, indeed, more "together" than you ever imagined.

What's more, you made an incredible journey to get to the human dimension, where you now have an important part to play. The possibilities for you in the HD are endless, and your footprint here is eternal because you are One. This is the "constant and constructive" truth about you. It is nothing new. Your soul has whispered this truth to you your entire life. What *is* new is that, perhaps for the first time, you are beginning to listen and remember.

33. "Nikola Tesla Quotes." Goodreads. Accessed February 20, 2023. https://www.goodreads.com/quotes/1133528-every-living-being-is-an-engine-geared-to-the-wheelwork

The Creation Cycle

It is the nature of One to create so, accordingly, such is your human nature. And there is certainly a lot of creation going on in the human dimension. First, there is the creation of you and all human beings, as the direct expression of One, with the *Five Steps of Human Creation*. Then comes the creation of everything else in the HD as the direct expression of *you* and everyone in yet another five sequential phases, which I have dubbed *The Creation Cycle*, consisting of Awareness, Understanding, Choice, Action, and Opportunity.

From the narrow perspective of the HD, it might seem unimaginable that you are One creating the world around you; that is, until you begin to put all the parts of this dynamic process together and see how it happens. The five phases of The Creation Cycle occur rapidly, simultaneously, and inconspicuously, countless times, every moment of every day.

- You create as you plan your activities at home and at work.
- You create as you play, paint, write, sew, workout, throw a softball, hit a tennis ball, shoot hoops, run, practice yoga, etc.
- You create with the words you speak, chat, email, or text to friends, family, co-workers, and anyone you meet.
- You create with the thoughts that you choose to think.
- You create as you drive your car, cook a meal, take a shower, and even as you sleep!

In truth, there is no time when you are *not* creating. The fuel that feeds The Creation Cycle is *energy*, including the infinitesimal energies of all 114 chemical elements on the periodic table that are the building blocks of material form in the HD.

The five phases of The Creation Cycle are shown below in Figure 9. Each phase plays a unique part in this infinite and eternal circle of life. We will take some time here examining the technicalities of how the parts of you—soul, body, mind—work together throughout these creative phases. I have erred on the side of including more detail, rather than less, to emphasize the importance of this synchronization, so please be patient as you take it all in. Since there is no actual beginning or end to this continuous cycle, we will jump into the sequence with *awareness* as our point of entry.

Figure 9
The Creation Cycle

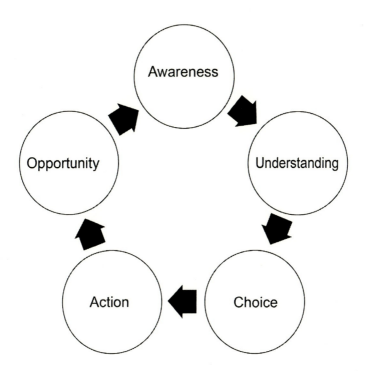

Awareness

It all starts with energy, vibrating at various distinct sub-frequencies. All this energy originates from the perfect and true absolute where it is unified and whole, resting in an inert and tranquil state, until it enters the human dimension as One: its dynamic and creative variant. This creative energy is the fuel for The Creation Cycle, and it shows up in the human dimension in three primary energy bandwidths: *form, movement,* and *possibility.* You were introduced to each of these briefly in Chapter 3 (see *The Major Polarities of the HD).* Now they are further elaborated in this overview of the phases of The Creation Cycle.

Like an antenna, your *awareness* is how you detect the vibrational ranges of each of these different energy bands in the human dimension. Awareness is how you take it all in. In other words, it is your *reception.* In every moment, all parts of you—soul, body, mind—work together to receive awareness.

There are three *channels* of awareness in the HD and, like a radio, each channel is especially attuned to one of the primary energy bandwidths. The channels of awareness are:

1. **sensing**—attuned to the energy of *form*
2. **emotion**—attuned to *the energetic vibration/movement of One*
3. **intuition**—attuned the energy of *possibility*

Collectively, the three parts of you collaborate, and calibrate, to channel your awareness of all the "stuff" of the HD through these three channels. You probably never thought of yourself as a human radio any more than you thought of yourself as a human light bulb but, here again, you are. You channel energy constantly, and each channel has a unique role to play in The Creation Cycle.

Sensing

Using your five senses—sight, hearing, touch, taste, and smell—you receive the energy of form originating from *taiji,* or formless energy. The sensing channel is activated when your body encounters the unique, energetic sub-frequencies of form within this bandwidth: *light, sound, solid matter, flavor,* and *odor,* each corresponding to one of the five senses. These energies are "picked up" in your body through their corresponding sensory *receptors: light* via *sight, sound* via *hearing, solid matter* via *touch*, and so on. In a high school science class, you may have learned to call this energy a *stimulus*, as part of the *stimulus-response* pattern of human behavior. Once received, your body spontaneously shares each sensation (or stimulus) with your mind, which helps evaluate and understand it.

While the sensing channel is activated, as it nearly always is, your body and mind jointly calibrate to the slower and more dense energy frequencies of form in the HD. Sensing allows you, through your body and mind, to interact with all other forms and beings in the HD because you all share the same energy bandwidth.

The collaboration between body and mind during sensing is palpable in the human brain as electrical impulses (yes, *energy*) produced by the sensory stimuli. These electrical impulses flow along the length of your brain cells (neurons) to your nerves as nerve impulses. Nerve impulses then stimulate your body's glands to release hormones, and the muscles of your body to respond. The electrical impulses enable your body and mind to interact with all the other beings and forms in the HD by sharing or exchanging energy. One obvious example of this energy exchange is the conventional handshake, which begins with the visual sensation of a hand extended toward you, triggering nerve impulses and hormonal release in your body, ultimately prompting your body's muscles to respond by returning your hand and making a tactile sensory connection between the two of you. Such actions were described as energy *transactions* in *The Quantum Truth* section of Chapter 6. Needless to say, this is one very simple example of the far more complex energy transactions you regularly experience with sensing.

While your mind and body are very active during sensing, your soul assumes the more passive role of impartial observer. Your soul is the part of you closest to One and the absolute and, from that broad perspective, it sees your body and mind as its offspring participating in a harmless game of sensing in the HD and has no judgment as to the outcome.

Emotion

The channel of emotion, as you might expect, is a bit more enigmatic than sensing. This is because emotion is the channel of awareness attuned to the energetic, pulsing, and vibrating *motion* of One in the human dimension. Interestingly, the word *emotion* comes from the Latin word *emovere,* meaning "to agitate" or "stir up," just as an act of kindness might *stir up* emotion, or you become *agitated* by a careless driver while out running errands. You know from personal experience that emotion is truly *moving.* Many common metaphors have captured this truth: rising emotions, waves of emotion, emotional high, emotional ups and downs, emotional roller coaster, etc.

Given that emotion is the energy of One, moving and flowing in the HD, it is no surprise that emotional awareness arises in the part of you that is closest to One—your soul. With emotion, your soul "surfs the wave" of One's vibrational current, then shares this energy with your body. You might have heard the expressions: "that was heavy," "emotional overload," or "full of emotion" to describe many of life's experiences when emotional energy augments the normal energetic composition of your body. When this happens, your body *senses* this new energy and prompts the brain to stimulate the nervous system, triggering your endocrine glands to release certain hormones. Suddenly you are "overcome with emotion," "paralyzed by fear," or have an "outpouring of love." This is how soul and body collaborate to impart awareness through the channel of emotion.

With emotion, your soul reminds you of your close connection to One and tries its best to translate that enormous truth into the diminutive realm of the HD through your body. Here, the worlds of the absolute and polarity collide, and you are left with the emotionally charged polarity of love-fear to sort things out in the next phase of The Creation Cycle.

Intuition

Intuition is the channel of all human possibility. When your awareness comes through this channel, your soul is, once again, an active participant, this time teaming up with your mind. When you *intuit*, your soul is showing your mind the vast array of possibilities for you, and all of humanity. Oftentimes, intuition appears as the foretelling of an event, such as a phone call or a personal encounter, or as a moment of "divine" inspiration when a new, innovative idea suddenly materializes.

With intuition, your soul and mind jointly calibrate to receive the energy of the highest, quickest frequency, thereby producing what has been called *extrasensory perception* (ESP). Intuitive awareness, then, is your mind's *extrasensory* (beyond the senses) reception of the bandwidth of all the possibilities the absolute has to offer. You might even think of intuition as one of your latent *superpowers*.

The challenge for your mind is what to do with all the extrasensory awareness that shows up with intuition. Once again, the worlds of the absolute and polarity collide. How can you wrap your mind around the enormity of the absolute from the narrow perspective of polarity? Your mind alone cannot begin to comprehend all the possibilities whispered to you by your soul. How can you accept your absolute superpowers when you see yourself as merely mortal? This is why you often ignore your intuition. You do not trust it. So, you resist following the "hunch" because you do not realize what is really happening when you *intuit*.

To the extent to that you allow yourself to trust your intuition, you benefit from its access to all the possibilities of the absolute. Interestingly, the origin of the word *intuition* sheds some light on this truth. *Intuition* comes from the Latin word *tuitionem*, meaning "to look after, care for, watch over, protect, and guard." Your intuition, then, is the channel of awareness that offers you the guidance and care of One in the HD, but only if you "tune in," trust, and accept it.

When you intuit, which is *always,* your body takes its turn as the passive observer. It takes no action, and senses only the brainwave activity from your mind's stimulation as it collaborates with your soul. Because of this, it often seems that intuition comes from "out of the body" instead of originating within you.

Understanding

After becoming aware of a particular energy by sensing, emotion, or intuition, the next step in The Creation Cycle is to *understand* what this energy means. Understanding is your *evaluation* or *interpretation* of awareness. With understanding you process, sort out, and assign meaning to the energy received through your awareness. In the human dimension this happens by assessing the relative difference between two points on a line. This is the way of polarity.

There are three *means* of understanding. Each relates to one of the channels of awareness, and each relies on one of the major polarities of the human dimension for its interpretation: *this-that, love-fear,* and *past-future.* These polarities were introduced in Chapter 3 as "The Major Polarities of the HD."

1. **thinking**—relates to *sensing* and *relies on this-that*
2. **feeling**–relates to *emotion* and *relies on love-fear*
3. **insight**—relates to *intuition* and *relies on past-future*

Here is a closer look at the part each one plays in The Creation Cycle.

Thinking

When you are thinking, mind and body work together to evaluate the various this-that relationships among the energetic forms of the HD that enter your sensory awareness, such as objects, people, symbols, images, colors, sounds, odors, words, and numbers. Obviously, you make these evaluations constantly. When you think, you measure, compare, and evaluate two distinct reference points (this-that) by applying *reasoning* to whatever has entered your sensory awareness to arrive at an understanding. Reasoning, sometimes called *critical thinking*, is the engine of thinking. Every second of your life is filled with reasoned evaluations.

With thinking, your mind understands that an *other* ("*not* you") energy form, or being, is present, then proceeds to evaluate the many this-that qualities of the other.

Accordingly, whatever your awareness senses, derives its meaning by comparing pairs of polar opposites. For example:

Day is brighter than night.

"And" is different from "or."

Warm cookies taste different than cold ice cream.

White is lighter than black.

Scream is louder than whisper.

Candy bar is sweeter than broccoli.

Rose is more fragrant than daisy.

This car is faster than that car.

Thinking (or, *thought*) is associated with the sensing channel of awareness because both sensing and thinking involve the mind and body. In other words, the mind interprets (understands) sensation by thinking about it. This is the natural *sensing-thinking* connection. The activity of thinking appears in the body as brainwave activity. This is the material, or bodily, outcome of your mind and body working together to understand the energy of form that enters your awareness through sensation. Because your body senses this brainwave activity, you naturally experience thought as occurring in your head, where the brain resides.

A popular metaphor that depicts understanding by thinking is the character of Lieutenant Spock in the classic *Star Trek* television series and movies. Spock is a Vulcan and Starfleet officer serving aboard the starship USS Enterprise. True to his Vulcan nature, Spock evaluates the precarious Starfleet predicaments and encounters by applying his superior reasoning or logical capabilities, absent emotion or intuition, an act which often aggravates his human Starfleet colleagues.

At this point in our evolution, thinking is our dominant means of understanding. This is the consequence of our strong identification with the body, as well as our constant preoccupation with all the this-that in the sensory world surrounding us in the great illusion of the human dimension.

Feeling

Feeling is a dialogue between body and soul. When you feel, body and soul work together to comprehend the prickly relationship between love and fear, the two polar opposite expressions of emotion in the human dimension.

It is important to distinguish *emotion* from *feeling*. These two words are often used interchangeably, but they have very different roles in The Creation Cycle. *Emotion* is your *awareness* of the energetic vibration and movement of One in the HD. *Feeling* is your interpretation, or *understanding*, of that emotional energy. Simply put, feeling is the understanding of emotion. You can have a wide variety of feelings, but they are all an attempt to understand the two basic emotions of love and fear, as depicted in Figure 10.

Figure 10

Emotions (Awareness)	
Love	**Fear**
Feelings (Understanding)	
Easygoing	Irritable
Pleased	Annoyed
Content	Unsatisfied
Calm	Restless
Accepting	Critical
Happy	Sad
Peaceful	Angry
Trustful	Jealous
Generous	Selfish
Enthusiastic	Bored
Encouraged	Frustrated
Confident	Ashamed
Merciful	Vindictive
Grateful	Unappreciative
Caring	Indifferent
Empathy	Apathy
Poised	Hysterical
Polite	Rude
Tolerant	Intolerant

Understanding the movement of One's energy in the human dimension is just as tricky as it sounds. To accomplish this feat, soul and body apply the standard of *fulfillment* to the two polar opposite expressions of emotion (*love-fear*), comparing that which is in harmony with and fulfills One (*love*), to that which does not (fear). It is no surprise that love is more fulfilling than fear, but the complexity arises because your soul enters this dialogue from the infinite perspective of the absolute, whereas your body is firmly grounded in polarity. The soul can easily discern the *love and fear* of an emotional situation, but the body just sees *pleasure and pain*. For example, you might feel angry and hurt about your firstborn's crusade to go to an out-of-state college when, in actuality, the underlying emotion is your parental fear of loss and separation from your child.

It is natural that feeling would focus on the understanding of emotion since feeling and emotion both involve the body and soul. This is the natural *emotion-feeling* connection. One familiar metaphor that represents understanding with feeling is the classic "gut feeling" or "gut reaction" to a situation. In these situations, because your soul shares emotion with your body, you often experience your feelings as occurring specifically in the body's central point—the pit of your stomach. Your gut feeling is the body's attempt at understanding the emotional energy of love and fear.

While feeling, the soul imparts its natural understanding of the Oneness of all, therefore feeling is especially focused on the connections, and energic transactions, between human beings. As evolving human beings, we struggle with the meaning of emotion and knowing when or how to use our heads (thinking) versus our guts (feeling) to understand life's emotional ups and downs. Despite this, because feeling involves both soul and body, and we so closely identify with our bodies, we have generally come to accept that, for better or worse, most situations are better understood by applying both thinking and feeling.

Insight

In a nutshell, *insight* is your means for deciphering your intuition. Like intuition, insight occurs with the close cooperation of mind and soul. With insight, your soul and mind team up to discover and understand the limitless possibilities of the absolute that enter your awareness as intuition.

In the human dimension, past-future are the two reference points used by your mind to understand in two parts what is truly only *one* present moment. The polarity of past-future allows your mind to evaluate the infinite possibilities from which you may choose to experience the present moment. Insight uses past-future as a way of separating and sorting out, not only events, but all manner of form in the HD, to give each meaning by comparing it to all others.

The understanding of insight hits you at the quickest energy frequency, like a "fast pitch," and holds more information than your mind can absorb and process with polarity alone. The magnitude of possibility within the realm of the absolute is simply too hot to handle. For this reason, we often misinterpret or mistrust our insight and, in doing so, miss out on the expansive awareness that comes with intuition. An example of insight are the moments of satyagraha that you might have experienced along this journey. The experience of the "force of truth" is your "fast pitch" insight at work.

Because polarity, itself, is inadequate for understanding the intuition that comes at us with such velocity, insight imparts *vision*—an instantaneous *seeing* and *knowing*. With vision, your mind can more readily accept and assimilate all the possibilities and mysteries of the absolute from within the limited framework of polarity.

Because both insight and intuition involve the soul and mind, there is a natural *intuition-insight* connection. Here, body takes a back seat, and does not get involved. Accordingly, insight appears to have an upward and outward focus that transcends the body. This is why you might experience insight as occurring outside or above your body, an idea which is sometimes comically portrayed as a light bulb above the head.

Figure 11

In our current stage human evolution, we strongly identify with our bodies, and since our bodies are not actively involved with insight, we often dismiss the vision of insight as an "overactive imagination" or "useless daydream." But insight is as innately human as thinking and feeling. When you trust your insight and accept the possibilities its vision holds for you, coupled with thinking and feeling, you are afforded a comprehensive understanding of the human dimension and its connection to the absolute. Having such a broad perspective boosts your general problem-solving ability, innate creativity, and overall well-being in the HD.

Choice

All your *thinking, feeling,* and *insight* culminates with a choice. *Choice* always follows understanding in The Creation Cycle, even when you do *not* choose, because to *not* choose is also a choice. Choice is the powerful expression of your free will. It is your personal stamp and ultimate decree as to what you will create. Ultimately, your choice determines what *action* you will take in the next step of The Creation Cycle.

Choice is a pivotal point in The Creation Cycle. Naturally, you make countless choices every second of every day. You do this out of necessity to continue creating yourself and everything that surrounds you in the HD. Some choices you are aware of and generally understand how you make them, for example:

- what to wear today
- what to eat for breakfast
- where to go on vacation
- whom to marry
- which job offer to take
- how many children to have
- whether to attend a particular event

Other choices you might be aware of but do not understand exactly how they are made:

- not touching a hot stove
- preferring blue over red
- following your normal commute to work
- balancing while riding a bike
- favoring one person over another

Then there are some life-sustaining choices that you make, which you are probably not at all aware of, nor do you understand how they occur. For example:

- breathing
- heartbeat
- cellular regeneration
- creating with polarity

These are just a few of the types of choices you make continuously, every day. Obviously, there is a lot of choosing going on. But how do these choices get made? Which part, or parts, of you is doing the choosing? To get to the bottom of who is really captaining the Good Ship *You*, we will take a closer look at how your choices are made.

Intention

With every choice you make, you introduce your own powerful creative energy into The Creation Cycle. This energy is your *intention*. Your intention is the force behind every choice you make. With your intention you shape the energies of *form*, *movement*, and *possibility*, which have entered your awareness through *sensing*, *emotion*, and *intuition*, and which you have come to understand with *thought, feeling*, and *insight*. Think of your intention as the electricity that operates the sawmill of choice, with which you carve out the entire human dimension.

The word *intention* comes from the Latin word *intendere*, meaning "to turn one's attention to," or, literally, "extend toward." And this is exactly what happens with your intention. When you choose, the creative energy of your intention turns its attention to, and extends toward, a form, movement, or possibility, and annexes it into your experience of the human dimension. True to the nature of polarity, your intention is expressed in one of two ways: *attachment* or *resistance*. For example, as you scan a room crowded with people, you might turn your attention (intention) toward (attachment) or away from (resistance) a particular person.

When intention is expressed as attachment, you extend your attention toward another point on a line of polarity and say: "yes." Attachment extends and latches on to something, such as a form, object, feeling, or another human being, and "holds on" or "pulls" it toward you. In the crowded room example above, you might focus on that person or go up to them and say "hello."

Intention expressed as resistance rejects or "dismisses" a thing and "pushes" it away. With resistance, you also direct and extend your intention toward another point on a line of polarity, but instead you say: "no." In the crowded room example, you might avoid the person or overlook them altogether.

We will revisit intention, attachment, and resistance again in Chapter 9 when we add another layer to your understanding of how they work together with polarity.

Soul vs. Ego

In the example above, you might be wondering which part or parts of you are doing the attaching or resisting and saying "yes" or "no" in your choices? In other words, what is the source of your *intention*?

When a choice is made, your body is generally passive, waiting to put your choice into action. However, a lively debate ensues between two strong voices within you about what to choose. These are the voices of your *soul* and your *ego*. Remember that your ego is the invention of your mind that causes you to see yourself as separate from others in the HD, whereas your soul is the part of you that fully experiences your connection to One and the absolute. You have heard these voices many times. Here is how the debate unfolds.

First up, your soul. Since your soul is your point of origin, formed before your body and mind were even conceived, your *true* nature is found in the part of you that is your soul. It follows, then, that your soul is the source of your *true* intention.

Your soul is always there for you in the HD. It has a quiet and unassuming presence because it is the part of you closest to One and the absolute and, therefore, has nothing to worry about or prove. It fully embraces the truth of the whole you and your connection to all human beings as One. Therefore, your soul is always cool and calm, regardless of the situation or whatever choices you make. But even though your soul has no judgment about the outcome of your choice, it does have a specific intention regarding your choices. That intention is *integrity*.

There's that word again. The word *integrity* comes from the Latin word *integrare* (to make whole) and has come to mean "wholeness" or "unity." This meaning is reflected in the intention of the soul, which is to impart integrity in two constructive ways. First, it intends to keep the three parts of you–soul, body, and mind–intact and viable in the HD. Your soul's intention is your life force. You can confirm this simply by noticing the everyday life-sustaining choices you make that you might not even be aware of, such as your breathing and heartbeat. In other words, it is your soul's intention to keep the Good Ship *You* afloat.

Second, and just as important, it is the intention of your soul to bring integrity to all the other choices you make, big and small, such as: *what to wear, what to eat, where to go on vacation, whom to marry, which job to take, and so on.* When making an *integrated* choice, all parts of you have a say in the matter. Soul, body, and mind leverage the benefits of *thinking, feeling,* and *insight* to arrive at an optimal understanding that best serves you. This integrated understanding is the basis of soul's *intention.* The degree to which a particular choice reflects the *wholeness* and *integrity* of your understanding, the better it will serve you and provide a more fulfilling experience of the human dimension. This is the key to your contentment and well-being.

For example, by choosing to read this book, you made an *integrative* choice to remember how the true parts of you come together to create your experience of the HD. You might even say that it was your soul's intention that you follow this path to remember the truth about you. Indeed, for my part, I understand that it was my soul's intention to provide you with this opportunity.

Now for your ego. Rather than being a true part of you, your ego is an invention of your mind and, unlike your soul, it is not invested in the viability of the whole you. And because it is confined to your mind, it lacks any innate awareness of the connection you share with all other human beings through your soul. On the contrary, it sees its only job as *self*-preservation—to perpetuate the illusion that you are separate from others.

Ego is easy to spot because it is loud and bossy. It could not care less about body and soul. In fact, it wants you to believe that you are *only* your mind and nothing more. It certainly does not want you to listen to your soul and remember who you truly are. Its goal is survival and, forever fearing its demise, tries to undermine the intention of your soul in the choices you make. This shows up in obvious *selfish* choices, like blaming others for your mistakes, failing to consider another person's point of view, or promoting personal gain at the expense of others.

Integrity and Choice

If you pay attention, you will hear the never-ending debate between ego and soul inside you. As you listen to these distinctly different voices, you can pick up on what is important and true. This is the ultimate example of what it means to "listen to you"—a key theme of this book. Choices made with integrity honor the Oneness of all things and endeavor to make them whole and complete again, just like One. These are the choices that cultivate the qualities of the absolute—perfect and true—within the HD. This is what your soul attempts to create with the choices you make, whether you are aware of it or not. Integrated choices are the endgame for you and your soul, and the direct path to your contentment and well-being. This is because integrated choices are anchored in the most comprehensive understanding of the truth about you and take into consideration how all of you (soul, body, and mind) relates to the HD and the absolute.

Of course, some choices you make are bound to be more integrated than others. This is to be expected because, as with all human beings, you are on a transformative path to remembering the truth of who you are. As we move beyond our evolutionary infancy, toward more fully remembering who we are, we will naturally become more proficient at making integrated choices that are better aligned with the perfect and true absolute.

Action

In the next phase of The Creation Cycle, your choice is expressed in the human dimension by your *action*. Action is your choice set into motion, powered by the energy of your intention. It is your action that propels whatever you choose out into the HD.

Action involves all three parts of you: soul, body, and mind. Some actions are directed *outward,* toward other people or things, wherein your body and mind work together; for example, walking, running, dancing, eating, sleeping, laughing, crying, working, writing, designing, building, growing things, throwing things, and playing video games. It also includes your more subtle, but no less impactful, facial expressions, eye movements, glances, touches, and, most notably, your words.

Other actions are directed *inward,* with your choices about how to think or feel. We have already established that thinking and feeling are the means for understanding your sensory and emotional awareness, but they are likewise actions that you choose. In other words, you can choose how to think or feel about any person, place, thing, or event that enters your awareness. While this idea sounds quite empowering, it is nothing new. You might have heard it described as "the power of positive thinking," "choosing your thoughts," or "changing your attitude." It simply means that The Creation Cycle not only impacts what surrounds you but also what comprises you.

Once you set your intention with your choice, unless it is altered, the creative energies of body-mind-soul collaborate to engineer the human dimension, including you as its inhabitant, in such a way that reflects your intention. They are helpless to do otherwise. Your intention is just that powerful. You are the engineer. In truth, you are both the creator and the created.

The most important thing for you to understand about the action phase of The Creation Cycle is that your choice, set into action, sends a current of energy throughout the entire human dimension in the frequency of a newly created form, movement, or possibility. These new creations are then available to be channeled with the awareness of everyone through their sensing, emotion, or intuition. With every action you take, the entire human dimension adjusts and changes, on a small or grand scale, depending on what you have chosen. Every act(ion) of your creation adds new creative energy for everyone in the HD and alters the HD forevermore. The next section of this chapter (*Opportunity*) offers an example of this dynamic process.

The action phase of The Creation Cycle underscores just how closely connected you are to all human beings and emphasizes the magnitude of your choices. Through your actions, you shape the energetic composition of the HD and create the human experience for you and everyone. In every moment, you create the HD that you inhabit. You dress the stage for your performance. You make the bed you lie in. This is the true law of karma.

Opportunity

There is one more very important phase of The Creation Cycle. *Opportunity* is the situation in which you find yourself or, more aptly, the *conditions* that provide your awareness. It is the hand you have been dealt to play and create with. It is opportunity that asks the question "now, what will you create?," which is ultimately answered with your choice. Now that you have a handle on the other four phases of The Creation Cycle, imagine for a moment that opportunity is where creation begins, even though you know that The Creation Cycle has no actual beginning or end point.

There are countless examples of opportunity in the HD, big and small, including:

A chance encounter

The traffic pattern during your evening commute

An email that shows up in your inbox

A new work assignment

A health update from your doctor

The offerings on a restaurant menu

Waking up to a new day

The birth of a new baby

The death of a loved one

The list of opportunities is endless because opportunity is everywhere in the human dimension, all the time, even now as you read this book. There is a markedly profound reason for the abundance of opportunity in the HD. It is because every opportunity is the sum of *all* actions, resulting from *all* choices, grounded in *all* understanding, originating with *all* awareness, of *all* human beings, throughout *all* history. Opportunity, then, is the product of all human creation, layer upon layer, since the dawn of humanity. Opportunity even includes what brought you here to this moment.

Take one example from the list above—the chance encounter. Here is how opportunity works. One day, you wander into the cookie aisle (choice, action) of your favorite (understanding) grocery store, and you come upon (awareness) a stranger who greets you with "hello" (action).

The fact this store even exists in the first place is the product of the awareness, understanding, choice, and action of many people who made it possible (investors, executives, designers, builders, etc.), and the fact that you show up there, in that moment, is due to the awareness, understanding, choices, and actions of many people, especially your own, which led you to this spot on this day (opportunity). Can you even imagine how many people contributed to the creation of this unique moment?

The stranger tells you (action) that she regrets (understanding) taking the last package of special gingerbread Oreos, and comments on how many different types of Oreos there are now to choose from (understanding). For a few minutes, you and the stranger reminisce (choice, action) about your memories of Oreos. She mentions (choice, action) that the absolute best Oreos are the homemade variety made at a local coffee shop nearby (understanding). You think about it (understanding) and decide (choice) to invite her (action) to join you at that bakery for homemade Oreos and coffee when you finish shopping. She deliberates (understanding), but accepts (choice, action) and meets you up the street for a cup of coffee and the world's best homemade Oreos.

In what appears as a mere chance encounter, the awareness, understanding, choice, and action of many people created this opportunity for you and a stranger to meet. Advancing this scenario, you and the woman date, break up with current partners, get married, and have a son who grows up to work for the peace corps, thereby influencing the lives of many throughout the world with his awareness, understanding, choices, and action. And this is just one tiny slice of the sum of *all* actions, resulting from *all* choices, grounded in *all* understanding, originating with *all* awareness, of *all* human beings, throughout *all* of history.

EveryOne

Opportunity is the creative product of all human beings universally and eternally in the human dimension. It is not just your individual situation, but the entire human condition. Opportunity is the never-ending story of humanity. It is the creative masterpiece of form, movement, and possibility of everyone, throughout all human history, created together by our collective awareness, understanding, choice, and action.

Everyone means each and every One in the HD. That is to say, *everyOne*. And while it is still all about *you*, in truth, *you* are much more than you have imagined. You are not just *you,* the individual. You are also the sum of *all* human beings together in the HD—the collective you, including your parents, children, friends, co-workers, those you briefly interact with, and even those you have never seen or met, near and far. You are *all* One. You are *everyOne*.

While opportunity is naturally abundant in every moment, it is also in a constant state of flux since it is the product of all the variable moment-to-moment choices of everyone in the human dimension. Therefore, the opportunity for what you might create is endlessly changing. You can easily see this as you go about your day and watch the world change before your eyes.

Your appointment is canceled

A co-worker becomes ill

It begins to rain

A bouquet of flowers is delivered to you

You run into a good friend on the street

You hear a favorite song

You may have noticed another paradox hiding within The Creation Cycle, seeing that it reflects both *determinism* and *free will*. You are presented with an opportunity, as *determined* by everyOne, then, with your personal choice, you exercise your *free will* with how you will contribute to the HD. It is everyOne, including you, who provides the opportunity—the *condition*—that enters your personal awareness for your choice so that, collectively, you might all move The Creation Cycle further along. You and everyOne constantly team up to create in tandem with every ordinary and extraordinary choice you make.

Full Circle

It helps to come full circle and recognize how all the *phases, channels,* and *means* of The Creation Cycle come together with the *steps* and *parts* of the Five Steps of Human Creation. This is an integrative approach after all. It is also, understandably, a lot of detail to sort out. But having a good grasp of how all the parts fit within the whole is essential for remembering the truth of *who you are, where you came from,* and *why you are here.* I have tried to break it down for you along the way, but it can still be difficult to visualize how all it all comes together. So, for the more visually inclined, Figure 12 illustrates how the parts of The Five Steps of Human Creation connect with the phases of The Creation Cycle.

Figure 12

FIVE STEPS OF HUMAN CREATION
One → Soul
Soul → Body and Mind
Mind → You and Your Self
Your Self → Ego and Other
Other → This and That

THE CREATION SEQUENCE (Five Phases)				
Awareness	Understanding	Choice	Action	Opportunity
Your Reception	Your Evaluation	Your Intention	Your Contribution	Your Situation
Channels	Means			

You	Channels	Means
Body-Mind	Sensing *Energy of Form*	Thinking *Uses Reason*
Soul-Body	Emotion *Energy of One's Movement*	Feeling *Uses Fulfillment*
Mind-Soul	Intuition *Energy of all Possibility*	Insight *Uses Vision*

At this point on your path to the truth of *it all,* hopefully you are beginning to remember the truth about *who you are* and *where you came from*. And with your new understanding of The Creation Cycle, you can begin to glean the answer to the third and final question of this journey: *why am I here*? So, next on this journey, we will get clear about the meaning and purpose of your life.

Sati Seven: Your Stories

1. Find your seat (refer to Sati One, if needed) and settle in.
2. Begin by taking a cleansing breath: a slow, deep inhale, holding it for a second, then exhaling with a gentle, but audible, sigh.
3. Repeat this cleansing breath another two times, then return to your breath's normal rhythm. Notice how you feel.
4. Now, turn your attention to the various sounds within earshot of your seat. Explore all the space around you, resting your awareness momentarily on each sound that you discover. Likewise, focus your awareness to the space within you and notice what you hear.
5. Spend about three minutes simply noticing all the sounds within your awareness. As you do this, observe the dialogue in your mind regarding each one.

    How many different sounds can you identify?
    What words do you use to identify each sound, i.e. air-conditioner, car horn, conversation, beathing?
    Which sounds are soothing? Which are annoying?
    Do you feel compelled to modify or prevent any sounds?
    What words or feelings do you use to bring understanding of each sound?
6. Then, relax your awareness and open your eyes.

The source of each sound that you identified here is a distinct pattern of energy moving through the air and within your body. Each energetic pattern is invisible to the eye but enters your awareness as sound waves via your sense of hearing. What distinguishes each one is the story you tell about it. For example, a passing train is an annoying

interruption for you, whereas to another person it might be soothing. The wind rustling trees outside worries you about the possibility of falling tree limbs, whereas it is pleasant for another. These are stories you create with your *understanding* of the energy entering your *awareness* as sound waves in The Creation Cycle. Your stories don't end with sound waves. All energy forms entering your awareness wait for you to give them a story with your understanding. In truth, just like sound waves, each form is simply pure energy. Pay attention to the stories you tell. It is the stories you create that determine your experience of the human dimension.

$$\bigcirc\!\!\!8$$

Experience

We are not human beings having a spiritual experience.
We are spiritual beings having a human experience.[34]
—Pierre Teilhard de Chardin

Who are you?
Where did you come from?
Why are you here?

These are the heavyweight questions posed at the beginning of this journey and echoed along the way. As an unwavering truth seeker, you have been rewarded with the answers to the first two questions. They are part of the truth you brought with you into this world and, until now, had likely forgotten. One final incredible answer awaits you to arrive at the whole truth. Your introduction to The Creation Cycle might have tipped you off to this one. The question is: *Why are you here?*

The answer is, again, astonishingly simple. So simple, in fact, that it might be hard to accept. But you do not have to accept it on faith alone. You need only to remember what you already know. That is, by witnessing how all the parts of the whole, absolute truth fit together. And since you are situated in the realm of polarity, it is only proper that this final answer comes in two parts: *meaning* and *purpose*.

---

34. "Pierre Teilhard de Chardin quotes." Goodreads. Accessed February 20, 2023. https://www.goodreads.com/quotes/21263-we-are-not-human-beings-having-a-spiritual-experience-we

Meaning and Purpose

At first, *meaning and purpose* might appear to be similar, especially in this context, where the *meaning* and *purpose* of life are often used interchangeably. But I am making an important distinction between the two. By *meaning*, I am referring to the activity, enterprise, or substance of your life in the human dimension. It is the *nature profonde* or "what the heck is going on here" of life. But the meaning of your life is only half of the answer to *why you are here.*

The other half of the answer lies in your life's *purpose*, that is, the product, outcome, or effect of life's meaning fulfilled. It is the *fait accompli* or the "mic drop" of life. For example, you could say the *meaning* of language is communication with words and symbols, but the *purpose* of language is its intended impact on its audience. Or you could say that the *meaning* of breathing is to supply oxygen to the body, whereas its *purpose* is to sustain life. Meaning and purpose work in tandem to provide the most comprehensive answer to the question: *why are you here?*

The Meaning of Life: Creation

One thing we can all agree on is the paradoxical truth that, in the human dimension, "change is constant." Change is nothing more or less than creation on display. In each moment, you and everyOne turn out multitudes of new creations, simultaneously, at breakneck speed, across overlapping phases of The Creation Cycle. Indeed, there is nothing going on in the HD that is not part of The Creation Cycle. There is no situation or event in your life that is not opportunity, awareness, understanding, choice, or action. Even when you believe you are not creating, you are merely creating in a different way. There is no exception to this. Just look around and observe this truth obviously displayed. Creation is "what's happening," and nothing more.

The essence of life is creation, and creation is the essence of life. How simple is that?

There is nothing you must learn.

There is nothing you must do.

There is nothing you must have.

There is nothing you must be.

Just create, and nothing more.

Nothing? *Really?* How can this be? This is not what you have been told.

What you have also *not* been told is that you already *know, do, have,* and *are* just fine. You are One. You are absolute—perfect and true. What more is there? What could One possibly require? Perfection lacks nothing. Let this be a comfort to you. You may *choose* to seek more knowledge; and you may *choose* to gain more experience; and you may *choose* to acquire more possessions; and you may *choose* to invent more versions of yourself, but there is *absolutely* no requirement for you to do any of this. *Why not?* Because it is *you* who also creates any requirement that you believe exists. It truly is all about *you.*

The Purpose of Life: Experience

If the meaning of life is to create, what, then, is the purpose of creation? The answer, again, is quite simple: the purpose of creation, and all human life, is to experience (observe, encounter, or undergo) whatever processes, events, or things you choose to create. The sheer experience of life is its utter purpose. In truth, it is the *absolute* purpose of life.

As One, you are the active, outward expression of perfect and true. Through you, the absolute experiences what it does not in its inert, whole, and undivided state. You make possible the experience of absolute perfection and truth in the human dimension, along with all the accompanying "this and that," "bumps and glides," "pleasure and pain," "darkness and light," etc., that come with polarity. The purpose of human life, then, is simply to experience the glorious nature of *absoluteness* through you and everyOne. This purpose is fulfilled when you remember who you are.

To be clear, the absolute lacks nothing. It has no *need* for your experience. When and how you choose to create and experience is entirely up to you, not part of some master plan or divine law. It is simply the nature of the absolute to express perfect and true, through One, and more particularly, through *you*. The only true master plan is that, for as long as you inhabit the human dimension, you create and experience.

This should come as no surprise. As past examples in this book have shown, you do exactly the same thing by creating experiences for yourself when you delve into a book, watch a movie, play a video game, etc. There is no requirement for you to have any of these experiences, it is simply your human nature to indulge in these pastimes as part of your experience of the HD. As it is with One, so it is with you.

The Ensō Circle of Life

Creation and experience. These are the final two parts of the whole truth. Together they reveal *why you are here*. The two go hand in hand, one always following the other. You create your experience, then you experience your creation. You go around and around in this true circle of life, as depicted in Figure 13-A. It is just that simple.

This circular trajectory, or "truth loop," shows up frequently, in many forms, within the human dimension. Most notable is the *ensō* circle, a sacred symbol with great significance in Zen Buddhism and Japanese calligraphy. The ensō circle can be traced back to sixth century Japan, where it represented the truth of the universal circle of vast space, lacking nothing and holding nothing in excess. Also known as the Affinity Circle, Zen Circle, and Circle of Togetherness, the ensō is painted with a single, fluid brushstroke, as depicted in Figure 13-B. Once it is drawn, it is not altered in any way, so as to honor the singular, present moment in which the mind frees the body to create.

The ensō may be a closed circle, signifying the perfect and true absolute, or partially open, representing the illusory imperfections along the path to remembering the truth. The ensō circle can also symbolize the nature of polarity, with the outer circle having no beginning or end, suggesting the immensity of the whole, satisfied, harmonious, absolute; whereas the inner core depicts the illusion of the human dimension contained within the absolute. This rich symbolism illustrates the polar opposite qualities of visible-hidden, simple-profound, and empty-full. In essence, the ensō circle is a simple and elegant representation of the absolute circle of life.

Figure 13-A

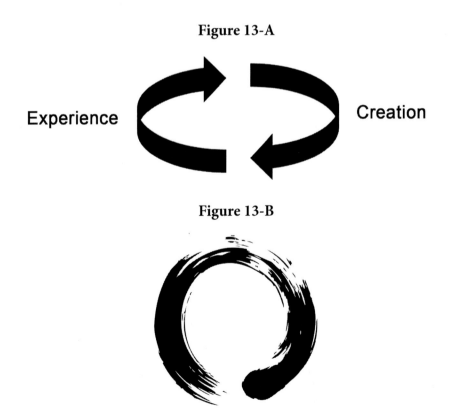

Experience   Creation

Figure 13-B

The HD is teeming with symbolic circles, which, along with the ensō, have provided inspiration for countless creations. Examples include the logos of various companies, such as Lucent Technologies and AMD/Ryzen, notable architectural designs from Stonehenge to Steve Jobs' Apple Park in Cupertino, California, the ceremonial exchange of wedding rings, circular meditative labyrinths, the moon phases, and even the rings of a tree trunk. Raise your ice-cold beer bottle and watch an ensō circle materialize on the counter in the bottle's condensation pattern. Cheers to a refreshing new Zen moment every time!

On this journey, you have seen different versions of the ensō circle, for example, in the circular phases of The Creation Cycle, the symbol of yin-yang, and now in the active, outward, "put it out there," yang energy of creation in rotation with the passive, inward, "take it all in," yin energy of experience. Creation and experience are intrinsically bound together in this loop; neither occurs without the other. Their relationship is essential to their existence.

And as you are about to discover, in the human dimension, relationships are the true key to life.

Sati Eight: Orchestra

1. Find your seat (refer to Sati One, if needed) and settle in.

2. Begin by taking a cleansing breath: a slow, deep inhale, hold it for a second, then exhale with a gentle, but audible, sigh.

3. Repeat this cleansing breath two more times, then return to your breath's normal rhythm. Notice how you feel.

4. This sati relates to *Sati Seven*, so be sure to have completed that exercise before proceeding here.

5. Now, turn your attention, once again, to all the sounds surrounding you in your seat. This time, use your shoshin beginner's mind and imagine that each sound is new to you, having never heard it before. Intentionally refrain from labeling or judging the sounds you hear. Try to experience them as the pure energy sound waves they are.

6. Next, imagine each sound as a distinctive musical instrument among the orchestra of all sounds, playing a song unlike any other you have heard.

7. Spend about five minutes with this exploration.

   Do you hear any rhythms or melodies arising among your sounds?

   Which "instruments" of sound are louder? Which are softer?

   Can you identify the more discreet sounds and appreciate what they contribute to the "orchestra?"

8. Finally, relax your awareness and open your eyes.

This sati exercise is an opportunity to experience the sounds within your immediate space in a new way, without telling the usual stories about them as you did in *Sati Seven*. Here, you are guided to an understanding of sound waves entering your awareness in a fresh, new way, without habitual judgments and labels, thereby intentionally creating your experience.

Relationship

Creativity is an inherent human quality of the highest order.
When we create, we become more than the sum of our parts.[35]
—Yanni

WITH A NEWLY SPARKED MEMORY OF THE MEANING AND PURPOSE OF your life, and how soul, body, and mind work together throughout The Creation Cycle, you are ready for a deeper dive into the inner workings of creation. This closer look will help clarify any lingering questions you might have about the mechanism of creation.

It is time to rediscover, or *remember*, how you create in *relation* to all other human beings, collectively, as everyOne in the HD. This is where the "parts" of *creation* and *polarity* come together. You could even say that there is a *relationship* between the two.

Relationships & The Creation Cycle

When you think of *relationships*, what likely comes to mind are your connections to other people, such as family members, friends, and romantic partners. But here *relationship* takes on a much broader meaning because what you are doing here in the HD, is not only creating relationships with people but with all energy forms—animal,

35. "Yanni quotes." Goodreads. Accessed February 10, 2023. https://www.goodreads.com/quotes/1226561-creativity-is-an-inherent-human-quality-of-the-highest-order

plant, mineral, liquid, gas, light, sound, thought, feeling, and so on. And you do it constantly. With every breath of air, casual glance, spoken word, and discreet gesture, you create the relationships that determine your experience of the HD.

When you consider the process of human creation, it is clear that your arrival in the HD is the result of a series of newly formed relationships between two points. First comes the relationship between the absolute and One, followed by One and your soul, then the soul and its offspring, body and mind, combining to form you. Upon your arrival in the HD, you begin creating all the things that you experience using The Creation Cycle, along with polarity. Polarity is a relationship builder in The Creation Cycle, responsible for the assemblage of distinct, polar opposite points connected by lines, as you might recall from Human Geometry 101 in Chapter 3. And while the *point* is the foundation of geometry and polarity, it is the *lines* connecting all the points that provide the framework for the human dimension. Lines are the scaffolding that hold it all together. Think of it as an invisible Tinkertoy set, like ones you may have played with as a child.

Figure 14

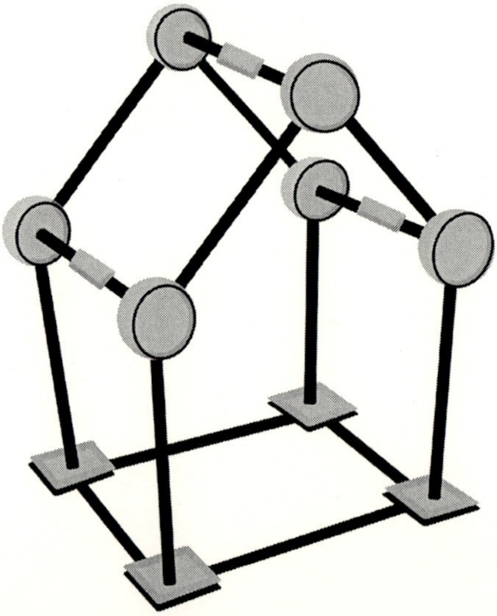

Each and every line that supports this elaborate framework is a *relationship,* representing both the difference, and value, between two points (i.e. objects, people, ideas, qualities, etc.), as well as an energetic link that binds them together. I sometimes refer to these as *relationship lines,* to remind you that that all relationships are lines connecting two points within the geometric fabric of the human dimension.

As you can imagine, there are countless relationship lines entering your awareness as energetic forms every second, waiting for you to understand and make a choice about what to create next. What you are invariably doing here in the HD, as you move through the phases of The Creation Cycle, is creating relationships. You are a master relationship builder.

Types of Relationships

The word *relationship* comes from a Latin word meaning, "bring back or restore," and in many ways, this is what happens when you form relationship lines. Because behind the creation of relationships is the intention of One to restore or *reveal* the qualities of perfect and true, within the HD. All relationships, then, are an attempt, using polarity, to recapture the singular, whole, and fully evolved state of that which only appears as divided in the HD.

There are four primary types of relationships in the human dimension. These are the relationships between:
1.   the absolute and the human dimension
2.   soul, body, and mind
3.   you and your self
4.   you and all other forms

These were all introduced in the previous chapters, but now let's look at them in the context of relationships.

The Absolute and the HD—*Your Core*

This relationship is at the core of who you are. The absolute enters the HD as *you* through a series of polarities, starting with its extension as One, followed by the expression of One as your soul. The latter is the first and original relationship in human creation.

Every soul is the direct expression of One, which, in turn, is the outward, active expression of the absolute. As One, you are the very special connector, or relationship line, between the absolute (Point A) and the human dimension (Point B). In this relationship, all the perfect and true qualities of the absolute are abundantly available to you. Imagine that. This relationship offers you an opportunity for profound serenity and well-being, and affords you the infinite potential of the absolute within the HD.

Soul, Body, and Mind—*Your Form*

Chapter 6 revealed the truth that you are a hologram of three primary energies—soul, body, and mind. Together these three energies provide you with a form, like a virtual avatar, to enter the HD and interact with all other forms and beings. In your form, your soul is the direct expression of One, and your body and mind are expressions of the soul.

As I have said, there is constant collaboration among the three parts of you from the moment you enter the HD. You exist in the HD, and continually move through the phases of The Creation Cycle, not only as the energetic hologram of soul-body-mind, but also as a bundle of relationships between these three parts of you. These are relationships that provide you with the experience of awareness with sensing, emotion, and intuition, and understanding by thinking, feeling, and insight. The choices you make with integrity—that is, honoring the wholeness of you as soul-body-mind—bring you the most contentment and well-being.

You and Your Self—*Your Illusion*

You might also recall from Chapter 6 that, upon arriving in the HD, true to your creative nature, your mind fabricated a polarity between you (Point A) and your self (Point B). Your self is like a reflection in the mirror enabling you to look upon and relate to you. It is here that you become both the observer and the observed, attempting to understand you, through the reflection of you in your mind. Your self, then, is your *relationship* with you. This fundamental relationship is necessary for you to exist in the HD. However, by now you might remember that, in truth, you are not only your self but the full expression of One as soul-body-mind.

If you are like most people, you are frequently preoccupied with the relationship between you and your self. This is the relationship that regularly prompts the time-honored existential question: *who am I?* As a truth seeker, you have undoubtedly invested considerable time and energy pursuing the answer to this question. The relationship between you and your self is the focus and fodder of the much psychological investigation, and the predominant theme of most *self*-examination on the therapy couch. Regrettably, this work often ignores the other significant relationships, discussed here, which likewise impact your overall experience of life. Those therapies which adopt a more integrated approach and, at their core, recognize and honor the whole truth about you, arguably offer the greatest path to contentment and well-being.

You and Other Form—*Your Diversion*

Recall that after the creation of your self, you then use polarity to both create and experience all that surrounds you in the HD using The Creation Cycle. You are consumed with comparing an infinite number of *this* (Points A) and *thats* (Points B). Truth be told, it is pretty much all you do, all the time. This constant focus only serves to bolster your ego's desire to protect the identity of your self, and reinforce the illusion that you (we all) are separate from each other, rather than connected as One and part of the absolute whole.

Obviously, all relationships between you and other energy forms are important, but it is your relationships with those whom you consider to be your loved ones that have the most influence on your experience of the HD. These are the relationship lines extending between you and points you identify as relatives, friends, and significant others. As you do this, you are undoubtedly aware that all other human beings are also equipped with a mind and very active ego, which sometimes adds a layer of complication and drama to these relationships.

Paradoxically, even though necessary for our individual material existence, those relationships that distinguish us from all other forms in the HD also serve to distract us from the truth about *who we are, where we came from*, and *why we are here*. We become so entangled in the stuff we create to fill up the world around us that it never occurs to us that there is something much bigger, yet simpler, going on here. The benefits of contentment and well-being come by looking beyond our self-induced diversions to remember the truth of it all. That is exactly what we are doing here.

Relationship = Energy

Relationships are not just imaginary geometric lines. They are true *rays* of vibrational energy providing a connective tension, like a tightrope, between every set of two points. You have probably heard of being "drawn to" someone or something "like a magnet." As it turns out, magnetic energy, or *magnetism*, is a useful analogy to help explain energetic relationship lines because, remarkably, you function very much like a magnet in relation to other forms in the human dimension. It might seem strange to first compare you to a light bulb, then a radio, and now a magnet. But all these examples point to the truth that you are, fundamentally, a being of pure energy. As Nikola Tesla once put it: "If you wish to understand the Universe, think of energy, frequency, and vibration."

When you bring two magnets close together, they either attract or repel each other. This is because magnets have a north and south magnetic polarity causing opposite poles to attract each other and similar poles to repel each other. Magnetism is produced by the spinning of electrons within the atoms of every substance. This movement generates an electric current and causes each electron to act like a microscopic magnet. In most substances, equal numbers of electrons spin in opposite directions, which cancels out their magnetism. But in substances such as iron, cobalt, and nickel, most of the electrons spin in the same direction. This gives the atoms in these substances strong magnetic energy, although they are not yet magnets. To become magnetized, another strongly magnetic substance must enter the magnetic field of an existing magnet. The magnetic field is the area around a magnet that has magnetic energy. This magnetic energy is observable as lines, or magnetic rays, as shown in the arrangement of magnetized iron shavings on the bar magnet in Figure 15 below.

Figure 15

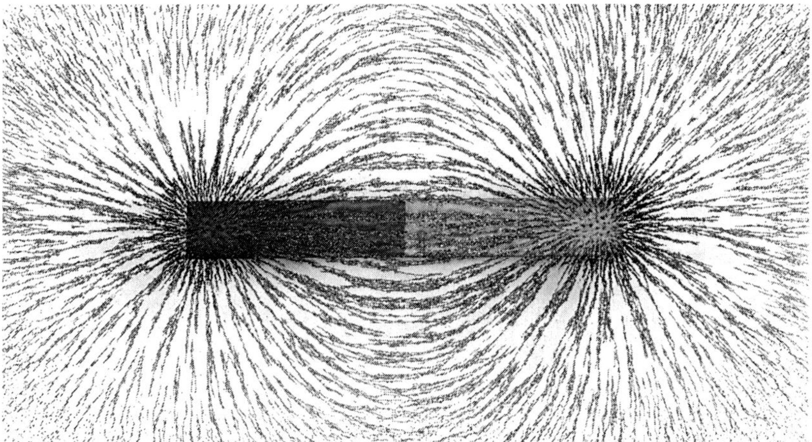

In geometry, a ray is a portion of a line that originates at a specific point and continues in a particular direction into infinity, as shown in Figure 16.

Figure 16

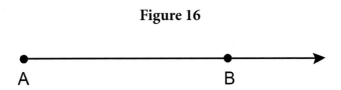

An inestimable number of rays might originate from any given point, especially when the point of origin is *you*, as in Figure 17.

Figure 17

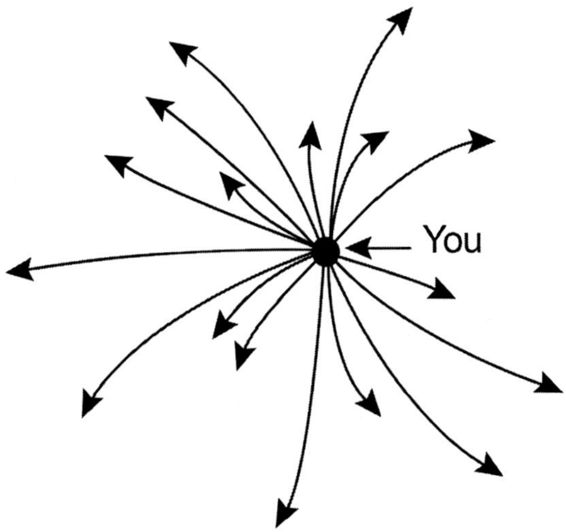

Do you see the similarity in the patterns of Figure 17 and the magnetic rays on the magnets in Figure 15? In truth, the point that is you (shown in Figure 17), and the points that represent all other forms in the HD, constantly emit an infinite number of energy rays, just like a magnet. These rays of energy are the relationship lines the link you to countless other points in the HD, as portrayed in Figure 18.

Figure 18

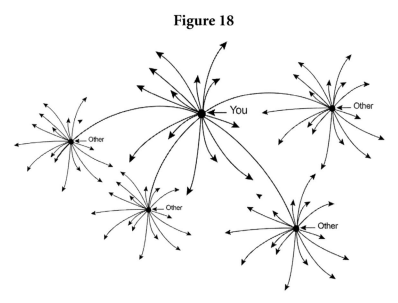

Just how does it happen that a Point B *magically* appears relative to Point A (you) to form a relationship line? Again, it is all about *you*. You are the conjurer and the magician. And your magic is to be found in the intention of your choice.

Thaumaturgy—You, the Wonderworker

Thaumaturgy is a word not often used in everyday conversation. It is typically defined as "wonderworking" and its practitioners are called *thaumaturgists, conjurers,* or *wonderworkers.* It comes from the Greek word *thaumatourgos,* composed with *thauma* (miracle) and *ergon* (work). In his book, *Authentic Thaumaturgy,* the notable pagan author, Isaac Bonewits, describes *thaumaturgy* as "the art and science of 'wonder working'; using magic to actually change things in the physical world."[36]

---

36. Isaac Bonewits, *Authentic Thaumaturgy.* 2nd ed. (Steve Jackson Games, 1998), 138.

Magic? *Really*? At first this seems far-fetched. Thaumaturgy is definitely not embraced by the mainstream of the human dimension. But, in truth, this is exactly what you do in every second of every day. It is another reason that you are *absolutely* wondrous. You are One. You are the wonderworker, conjurer, and creator of the HD. While this all sounds very mystical and supernatural, it comes as naturally for you as breathing, which, if you think about it, is rather wondrous itself. How, exactly, do you perform this wonderworking? You do it with the "magic" of your *intention* to conjure up points and establish relationship lines. This is just one of your everyday, basic, and natural superpowers.

Attachment and Resistance

It is the "magic" of your intention that brings polarity and The Creation Cycle together. With every choice you make in The Creation Cycle, big or small, you use the energy of your intention to mold the energies of form, movement, and possibility in the human dimension. Intention is expressed as either *attachment* or *resistance*. (See *Choice*, Chapter 7.) Attachment is the affirmative—pulling a thing to you, whereas resistance is the negative—pushing a thing away. Both types of intention appear regularly in the HD as *opinion, preference* or, more emphatically, *need*.

Resistance is attachment in reverse. When you resist a specific point, position, quality, outcome, etc. it is your resistance that solidifies its being, because how can you resist something which you do not first experience? Paradoxically, the more you resist something, the more you invite it into your experience. This truth was affirmed by the renowned Swiss psychotherapist, Carl Jung, when he said: "What you resist, persists."[37]

---

37. "What You Resist, Persists." *Well Being*. September 6, 2019. Accessed February 19, 2023. https://www.wellbeing.com.au/wild/what-you-resist-persists-10-ways-overcome-resistance

Resistance and attachment operate within the bounds polarity because when you resist or attach, you form a *u-axis* between *you* (Point A) and *other* points of your choosing (Points B). (See *The U-axis,* Chapter 3.) This u-axis is a relationship line connecting you to all the points, lines, planes, forms, and space that you have chosen with the power of your intention. With each new line of intentional energy, a new *relationship* is formed. As you do this, you "seal" your choice and—*boom*—something new appears for you in the HD.

Attachment and resistance comes quite naturally for you. They accompany your every choice in The Creation Cycle, including what to eat, what to wear, how to spend your money, romantic liaisons, political affiliations, and the sports teams you cheer for. You attach, resist, and form relationships countless times, every second, whether you are aware of it or not. Here are just a few examples of what this looks like in the HD:

the glance that reveals something new to you

a belief that some event will happen as usual

your worry that something you dread will occur

a word that arouses a feeling

any action taken by you that engages the energy of another

the delay or avoidance of an activity you fear

a new idea that reveals new possibilities, pleasant or not

the way you choose to understand another person or situation

a message you send to someone you know

a message you receive from someone you don't know

these ordinary, everyday thoughts or statements:

"I love my job."

"I want to get married."

"That driver is a jerk."

"I want to sell my house and move to another city."

"My children don't appreciate me."

"I want Thai food for dinner."

In each of these examples you conjure up a new form (object, person, event, feeling, idea, understanding) and begin a relationship with it. As you read through this list, do you begin to recognize what you are doing and how it all works? If so, you are beginning to remember what a wonderful thaumaturgist you are.

Let's add another fascinating layer to this truth. From the standpoint of the HD, it *seems* as though you bring everything into existence with The Creation Cycle, using your choice and extending a relationship line (u-axis) to some other point with attachment or resistance. And while this *is* true from the perspective of the HD, it is not quite the *whole* truth. From an absolute point of view, you do not *truly* create anything. Everything that is, and might be, already exists within the infinite realm of the absolute. It is simply hidden from you, waiting for your identification. The word *identification* comes from the fourteenth century Latin word *identitas* meaning "oneness" or "sameness." Your identification, then, is a recognition and confirmation of the truth of your *oneness* with all form, hidden and revealed, old and new, realized and possible, in the HD, as if a part of you that you did not know existed is being revealed. Your creations, then, are really *revelation*!

Astonishingly, this means that everything you experience in the HD already exists. It just sits there, in the realm of absolute possibility, waiting for you to identify it, throw it a lifeline with your attachment or resistance, and pull it into in the present moment of your experience. You, One, the wonderworker, bring to life all that you experience in the HD simply by identifying what is already there and creating a relationship with it. You do not create new stuff; you simply create relationships to stuff that already exists. You conjure it by revealing it. In terms of polarity, you provide the *u-axis* (relationship line) to all things that appear in your life in the HD. This is your magic. Satyagr-*aha!*

Science and Thaumaturgy

If the idea of magical powers still makes you nervous, perhaps you can take comfort in the hard sciences—specifically, quantum physics—which we have already discussed. (See *The Quantum Truth*, Chapter 6.) Quantum physicists would never consider magic to be the subject of their study, but this rapidly evolving field *does* merge the concepts of *form*, *energy*, and *relationship* and helps explain how the realm of the absolute connects to the human dimension. Quantum physics makes *you* the center point on the relationship line between the human dimension and absolute and explains how your relationship to all the other stuff of the HD effects your experience. Through the work of many notable physicists, including Einstein, Planck, Bohr, Heisenberg, de Broglie, and Schrödinger, the following evidence has come to light:

- Materialism, objective reality, and particle theory are increasingly being replaced by consciousness, observer-based reality, and wave theory.
- Wave theory, at its core, has shown that what really *is* is energy, behaving as waves, not particles or matter.
- Even more *magical* is that the energy waves surrounding you in the HD are shaped by your relationship to them throughout the five steps of The Creation Cycle, most notably, the *intention* of your choice. As such, these energy waves are part of your identity. You are One with them.
- And finally, Bell's theorem and the Aspect-Gröblacher experiments have demonstrated the *nonlocality* of reality, meaning that you do not create the human dimension alone. You do it in concert with all other human beings—as *One*.

Regardless of how you get there—magic or science—the truth is inescapable. You are wondrous. You are One. That is the truth about you.

The EveryOne Channel

Now you can comprehend the framework, or system, within which you create a personal relationship to everything you experience in the HD. This is true, not only for you, of course, but for *all* human beings—in other words, everyOne. Now envision everyOne as billions of points within the human dimension, nearly eight billion currently on Earth alone, each point emitting infinite rays of energy, forming countless relationship lines throughout the HD, as depicted in Figure 19. This vast network of relationships, the collaborative of human creation, provides you and everyOne with opportunities in The Creation Cycle and shapes your experience of the HD.

Figure 19

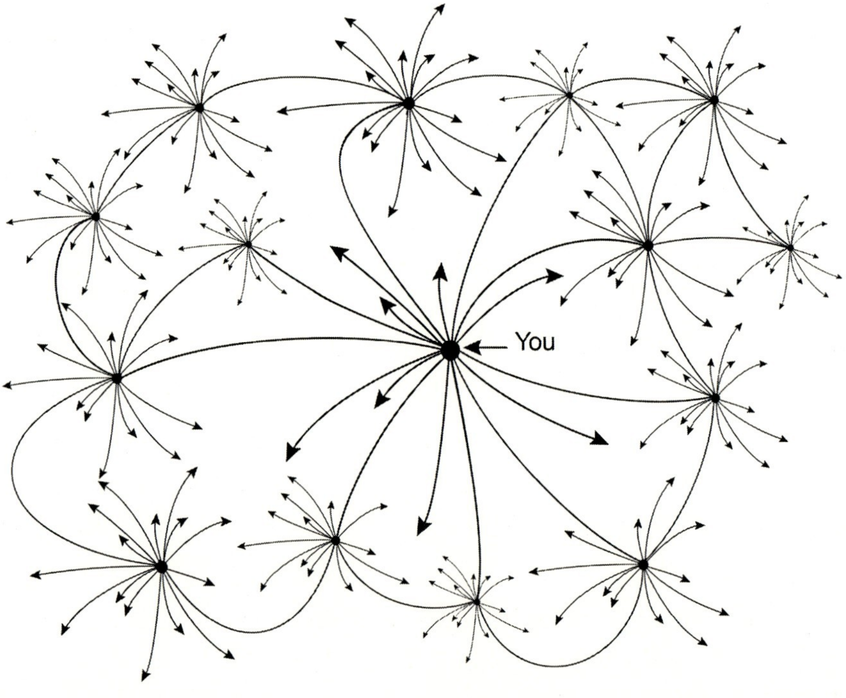

You, everyOne, and all the stuff of the HD are energy forms calibrated to the same, shared bandwidth, so you can think of this network as our common channel or "chat room" where everyone is "tuned in" or "logged on" and connected. This common channel is what allows you to mix, mingle, touch, collaborate, plan, organize, share experiences, and generally relate to all others in the HD. The HD is truly the *everyOne channel.*

Tuned into the everyOne channel, you and everyOne create together, continuously, in countless ways, swiftly moving through all phases of The Creation Cycle. With every new choice you make, your resulting thought, feeling, or insight leads to an action which hurls your creation out into the HD as a new energy form. The vibration of this new energetic form is broadcast throughout the HD, like a droplet of water hits the pond and sends a tiny wave of current throughout. This new wave of energy, originating with your creation, enters the awareness of others as sensory, emotional, or intuitive energy, providing a new opportunity on which they may, in turn, act. This is the "concert of life," in which you and everyOne tuned to the everyOne channel orchestrate the countless everyday experiences of the HD for everyOne, and in which everyOne is touched by the melodies of all others.

Community

The truth about the everyOne channel, and its effect on the human dimension, has been told many times, in many ways, throughout human history. Hinduism and Buddhism have given us the principle of *karma,* suggesting that our actions influence our future. The Christian Bible tells us that "whatsoever a man soweth, that shall he also reap."[38] Modern science offers the law of "cause and effect," in which one event contributes to a future related event. Even our common, everyday vernacular asserts: "You get what you give."

---

38. Galatians 6:7 KJV

The relationships that we create together in the HD form the basis for an expansive and interconnected community where a single ripple can be felt by all. It is telling that the word *community* originates from the *PIE* words *ko-* ("together") and *mei-* ("change"). It seems our earliest ancestors had the right idea about the meaning of life—to change together. Change is, after all, the experience of creation. Today, we call this inherently human enterprise *community*.

Community, in this context, does not only mean living in close proximity, like a neighborhood, although that might be the case. It refers to human beings coming together to create change with an awareness of our relationship to, or Oneness with, all others. Evidence of our fledgling, but growing, awareness of community can be seen in our retail co-ops, community gardens, animal protection groups, pet adoption organizations, neighborhood watch programs, community education, and even government sponsored programs, such as mandatory schooling, infrastructure improvements, Medicare/Medicaid, social security, and public safety initiatives. Community, then, is the platform for how we change together by leveraging the relationships created by everyOne in the human dimension.

Community begins with the absolute. Your entire experience emerges from this single, cohesive, and abundant source of perfect and true. Working together to engender a "community of the human dimension" provides everyOne the opportunity to experience these absolute qualities from within the illusion of polarity. But cultivating a community is not the only way to get to the absolute. Fortunately, the absolute is ubiquitous—everywhere, always—and its nature is to reveal the interconnectedness and wholeness of all things, especially its connection to you. It expresses this natural affinity in the human dimension with *grace*.

Sati Nine: Light Beam

1. Find your seat (refer to Sati One, if needed) and settle in.
2. Begin with a comfortably deep sama-vritti breath—inhaling to the count of four, then exhaling to another count of four.
3. Repeat this balanced breath five times, then return to the normal rhythm of your breath. Notice how you feel.
4. Now, gently open your eyes and instead of focusing your breath, turn your attention to all the "stuff" in the space around you, for example, table, chair, plant, picture, vase, floor, celling, wall, tree, sky, etc.
5. Scan this space, and briefly hold your gaze on each of the things within it, large and small. Use your shoshin mind and imagine that your awareness of each object is like a beam of light that reveals it to you as you turn your attention toward it, as if it were a flashlight exploring a dark room.
6. Spend about two minutes scanning the space around you with your imaginary beam of light.
7. Finally, relax your awareness and open your eyes.

Your beam of light is not imaginary. It is an example of the rays of energy that connect you to each form within your scope awareness, demonstrating you in relationship with all that is. Although scanning your surroundings with your light beam might seem rather common and unremarkable, it illustrates your special powers of thaumaturgy.

Grace

I do not at all understand all the mystery of grace—only that it meets us where we are but does not leave us where it found us.[39]
—Anne Lamott

Who are you?
You are One—appearing in the human dimension as a hologram of soul-body-mind energy.
Where did you come from?
As One, you are the active, outward expression of perfect and true, originating with the absolute.
Why are you here?
Your life is creation in action, and your purpose is to experience whatever you choose to create.

On this journey, you have witnessed these simple parts come together to tell the whole truth about you. It *is* just that simple, and it *is* all about you, even if you do not yet fully remember or embrace this truth. Any greater complexity arises only from the illusive layers of polarity and a desperately insistent ego. Whether you consider yourself to be a bona fide truth seeker or not, these are the questions that, if you do not sufficiently answer, you remain adrift in the human dimension and detached from your life's meaning and purpose. Every human being

39. "Anne Lamott Quotes." Goodreads. Accessed February 20, 2023. https://www.goodreads.com/quotes/6476160-i-do-not-at-all-understand-the-mystery-of-grace--only

needs a theology. As the philosopher-poet, John O'Donohue once put it: "If we stay trapped in the merely visible, we will never inherit our lives."[40]

Once you remember how all the parts fit together and how life really works, and you realize the simple meaning and purpose of your life, any lingering questions you might have must be related to how to live as One, an absolute being, within the human dimension. In other words, how do you use what you have remembered to:

enhance your personal contentment and well-being

answer life's biggest questions and navigate your toughest challenges

transform your world into a more habitable and user-friendly place

make choices that create a more joyful and fulfilling experience for you and everyOne

You have seen this list before. It was introduced in the "What's in it for me?" section of Chapter 1. Having taken this journey, chances are you might view this list differently now than when you first read it. If so, then it is a sign that you are beginning to remember the truth of it all.

What happens next is up to you. On one hand, you could do nothing and just accept that you will ultimately be just fine because, after all, you are One. Of course, that is true. On the other hand, now that you are empowered to create as you choose with The Creation Cycle, you might choose to create a more satisfying and joyful experience of the HD because, by remembering who you are, you are rewarded with a new understanding upon which to base your choices.

You also know that this is not always easy to do. Perhaps you have already encountered some fairly conspicuous roadblocks to creating differently, and even a few barriers to fully remembering *who you are,*

---

40. John O'Donohue, *Wisdom from the Celtic World: A Gift-Boxed Trilogy of Celtic Wisdom.* Audio CD, (Sounds True; Unabridged edition. July 29, 2005), "The Invisible World."

where you came from, and *why you are here.* Some of these obstructions might look like this:

> *I do not want to change. I am satisfied with how things are.*
> *Life is supposed to be difficult and filled with challenges—that is how we learn and grow.*
> *None of this matters to me. It is not important.*
> *I am skeptical. Where is the proof?*
> *It takes too much time and effort to understand and apply all this to my life.*
> *I trust my family, faith leaders, or scripture to tell me the truth.*
> *I worry about the consequences of changing my beliefs.*
> *I will wait for the scientific evidence to tell me the truth.*

Does any of this sound familiar? If so, then you are presented with yet another opportunity to moderate the ongoing debate between your *ego* and your *soul,* a regular contest recounted in Chapter 7, in which your ego's motive is rooted in fear and self-preservation, whereas your soul's intention is the pursuit of integrity and creativity.

Here is the bottom line. It is always your *choice* about how you *act* upon the *opportunities* entering your *awareness* for your *understanding* in The Creation Cycle. You have the final word on whether to create more of the status quo or create a more blissful experience. And while it is true that, regardless of what choice you make, you are going to be just fine, if you opt for the status quo, you may not be able to sustain the *understanding* that you will be just fine. That is the catch.

Thankfully, you do not have to go about the business of remembering and creating the experience of contentment and well-being alone. In the HD, you are regularly offered opportunities to remember the whole truth about you, inviting you, even compelling you at times, to create differently, that is, with integrity. In the HD these opportunities show up as moments of *grace.*

The Nature of Grace

Grace is typically defined as a divine gift, often bestowed by the virtues of beauty, kindness, and harmony. I accept this definition and broaden it by describing *grace* as what happens when the absolute gently pierces the illusion of the HD with the qualities of perfect and true, and nudges you toward living as One—a fully integrated being of soul-body-mind.

Grace is, indeed, a divine gift, given by One, meaning *you*, to *you*, from the part of you that is your soul, since your soul is the part of you closest to the absolute. With grace, One fulfills its intention to nurture and sustain you in the human dimension and satisfy your every desire on the "What's in it for me?" list above.

Simply put, *grace* is the "feel good" experience of the absolute in the HD.

Grace in the Human Dimension

Grace abounds in the human dimension. However, it is often unrecognized, misunderstood, or completely ignored. It regularly appears in the above-mentioned qualities of *kindness, beauty,* and *harmony,* each, in its own special way, nurturing and caring for you by revealing the perfect and true in the HD and guiding you to greater well-being.

You know you have been touched by the kindness of grace when, in a difficult moment or situation, another person unexpectedly shows up to care for you, or when you are simply offered a helping hand. It might seem as though an "angel" appeared for you in the form of a supportive friend or kind stranger. Or maybe it was you who was the angel when you stepped in to care for another. Kindness reflects the qualities of the *absolute*—perfect, complete, fulfilled, and utterly evolved. It asks for nothing in return because what could the absolute possibly ask for?

With the pure intention to nurture and care for you, kindness is simply a *giver* in the relationship between you and the absolute.

Graceful beauty is everywhere in the human dimension. It can be found in art, music, poetry, the human form, and all manner of design. *Merriam-Webster* tells us that beauty "gives pleasure to the senses" and "pleasurably exalts the mind or spirit" (soul). Nowhere is this more evident than in nature. It is well known that the beauty of nature nurtures us. Have you ever experienced a greater sense of calmness and peace while walking through the park, hiking through the woods, or strolling on the beach? The obvious benefit of nature's beauty is widely embraced among urban planners, who have long incorporated natural parks and green spaces into their designs. In the 1950s, the Japanese formally introduced the practice of *shinrin-yoku*, or "forest-bathing," after it was proven that absorbing the forest atmosphere with a walk among the trees restored absolute harmony and balance by calming the nervous system, reducing stress, and boosting the immune system.

While grace naturally appears in many ways throughout the human dimension, you may also cultivate grace in your life intentionally by acting upon what you have remembered here about *who you are, where you came from,* and *why you are here.* What follows are five practices for manifesting grace in your everyday experience. Each focuses on how your soul, body, and mind work together in The Creation Cycle. These five practices are opportunities for you to apply what you have remembered here in a meaningful and impactful way. *Practice* is the operative word, since each requires some reiteration and resolve to make it a regular habit and receive the advantages of grace.

1. Embrace Who You Are

First things first. It begins with remembering that you are One. But to fully embrace who you are means intentionally acting upon this truth in all the phases of The Creation Cycle as you create your experience of the human dimension. Embracing who you are is a momentous and difficult choice to make, but it is the key to inviting grace into your experience.

Let's do some soul-searching. Literally. To embrace who you are means accepting that you are much more than what you appear to be in the HD. There is an absolute quality to your being that begins in the part of you that is your soul. At your core, you are fundamentally and undeniably perfect and true, which is to say, *complete, whole,* and *eternal.* Yes, even godlike. To say this sounds like a lot. And in some ways, it is. It is the extraordinary truth about you.

I get that this can be difficult to hear, let alone embrace. Most people are far more accustomed to hearing that they are *unimportant, defective, inadequate,* and *ephemeral.* That is because most of your experience in the HD has conditioned your mind to believe that you are "less than" and "separate from" One. In fact, the three most authoritative institutions of the human dimension operate on the assumption that there is something inherently *wrong* with you. Here is what they tell us:

Religion: [Christianity]: You inherit "original sin" from the "fall of man" and must be forgiven and saved to reach heaven and be with God. [Judaism]: You are naturally inclined to disobey God's laws (sin) from birth. [Islam]: All are fallible with a latent capacity to sin, which requires Allah's forgiveness. [Hinduism]: Human nature is a combination of goodness, passion, and ignorance resulting in all manner of confusion and transgression in this world.

Science: You are a material body, perhaps with a mind, to the extent your mind is an operative of your brain. You function like a machine, with no demonstrable soul or any connection to a greater power, *if* one even exists.

Government: You are "in it to win it." The game is "survival of the fittest." You are fundamentally greedy, selfish, and egocentric, therefore prone to harm others who interfere with your agenda. A code of laws and law enforcement is necessary to deter you from, and punish you for, injuring others and even yourself.

Ouch. These are the subtle, and sometimes not so subtle, messages which have been scattered throughout the HD emphasizing that, on the polarity of "good-bad," you definitely tend toward the "bad," and certainly lack any divine origin. This negative programming has served only to reinforce forgetting your perfect and true nature and has likely caused you to espouse a rather cynical view of who and what you are. It is no surprise, then, that you are not very confident about understanding yourself to godlike, especially like any god you have known until now. And, in truth, you are not. You are certainly *not* the sort of god that has been promulgated by traditional religion. So, set the word *god* aside. Forget that misconception.

You are One. By embracing this truth, you gain the advantage of understanding the world differently. You remember that you are the expression, the appearance, and the event of perfect and true in the human dimension. In truth, you are what we consider to be "good," through and through, to the core of your being. More importantly, you are free to act upon this new identity by infusing The Creation Cycle with integrity and creating a new world of contentment and well-being. Embracing who you are compels you to do no less. Such a world was beautifully foretold by the celebrated scientist, theologian, and philosopher, Pierre Teilhard de Chardin, when he wrote:

The day will come when, after harnessing the ether, the winds, the tides, gravitation, we shall harness for God the energies of love, and on that day, for a second time in the history of the world, man will have discovered fire.[41]

2. Recognize EveryOne

Namaste. This Sanskrit word literally means "I bow to you." Over the years, it has become popularized as a salutation in the practice of yoga, where it has come to mean "the divine light in me greets the divine light in you." Of course, it is much easier to bow to someone's light than to their *darkness.* However, just like you, others often hide their light with their forgetful choices that lack the integrity of soul-body-mind. When this happens, it is easy to jump to the conclusion that they are "bad" people. But by embracing the truth that you are One, you are free to understand, choose, and act according to the truth that there are no bad people, only "bad" choices made by those who have forgotten who they are.

It is your nature, as One, to remember who everyOne is, in those shining moments when the truth of who they are is evident, and on the somber occasions when they linger in forgetfulness. In both circumstances, "namaste" must convey: "My soul recognizes your soul and remembers we both are One." When you remember and relate to everyOne as they truly are, you gently inspire others to remember the truth for themselves. After all, when your leg falls asleep, don't you wake it up so that your whole body functions with integrity as intended? Similarly, when you regard another as One, even when they are acting forgetfully, you help awaken them to the truth of who they are so that they might function with integrity as intended. You become the quiet whisper of truth for them. An act of grace from you, such as this, benefits you and everyOne in the human dimension.

41. Pierre Teilhard de Chardin, "The Evolution of Chastity," essay in *Toward the Future.* (Boston: Mariner Books, 2002), 86-87. https://archive.org/details/TowardTheFuture/mode/2up?q=someday.

Easier said than done, right? You know this practice requires patience. Remembering the truth of everyOne can be more difficult than embracing the truth of who you are. To begin with, not every person wants to remember who they are. Many people prefer to dwell in the illusion they have come to believe in. As a truth seeker, you might choose to remember the truth, but not every human being is as devoted to the truth as you. That is okay. Still, namaste to them.

In particularly tense encounters it may be tempting, even seemingly justified, to "fight fire with fire" and retaliate. This egocentric approach, however, only compounds forgetfulness with more forgetfulness. These situations require special handling. Let the illusion of polarity work for you. Since everything in the human dimension arises only in contrast to that which it is not, forgetting is understood only by comparing it to remembering. It is the relative difference between these two points that reveals the whole truth. Give them a satyagraha moment of incontrovertible truth. As an alternative to their forgetting, plant the seed for others to remember who they are by modeling the act of remembering who you are. Live by example. Be the change you want to see.

Imagine what the human dimension would look like if everyOne, or even a simple majority, remembered the truth of *who they are, where they came from,* and *why they are here*? Singer-songwriter John Lennon painted this picture beautifully with the lyrics to his famous song "Imagine," in which he describes a world transformed by living as One. Namaste, John.

3. Choose with Integrity

The meaning of life is creation, and as One, you are an active, energetic creation machine. Every day, along with keeping your body alive and functioning (no small task in itself), you constantly move from one place to another, tackle routine tasks, check off items on your "to-do" list, solve new problems, acquire more stuff, manage different people and situations, gain more experience, and create yourself anew. You do all this and still probably think it is not enough. This is the daily grind of The Creation Cycle. This is *you* in action, rather *many* actions, based on the choices that you make every moment. Some of these choices are significant and life changing. Most are trivial and mundane. Sometimes you are aware of your choices. Other times you are not. Regardless, you are incessantly making choices in The Creation Cycle.

How you make choices greatly affects your experience of life. When you *intentionally* choose with *integrity*, that is, with regard to the *whole* you—soul-body-mind—you create an experience of the human dimension that is pleasant and satisfying for you and everyOne. These are the *graceful* choices. Depending on your religious upbringing, you might even say that these choices create a little "heaven on earth." On the other hand, when your choices lack integrity, you create an experience of the HD that is, at best, uncomfortable, and in the worst case, painful, or which you might call *hell*. As mere constructs of the Abrahamic religions, heaven and hell are not places where we go, but experiences we create in the human dimension, whether just for ourselves or for everyOne.

How do you bring a little "heaven" instead of "hell" into your experience? You do this by recognizing, balancing, and *integrating* all parts of you—soul-body-mind—so that your choices better reflect the whole you. It is like giving yourself a cosmic "tune up" to realign you with the perfect and true. The first step of this energy realignment is to remember that your true nature, and the source of your intention, is to be found in your soul. This sounds simple enough, but remember, while it is your soul's intention to honor all parts of your being in making your creative choices, it is in no rush to do so, because it has no relationship to time. It knows you will get there eventually, so your soul has no strong opinion about your choices.

Thanks to your ego, the *whole* of you has a greater sense of urgency than does your soul, alone. This is when (and *why*) you introduce grace. In the moment of an important choice, practice focusing your awareness on all parts of you and become the *watcher* of the *whole* you. As you do this, tune in and listen to the debate between your soul and your ego. Notice that your soul calls for a choice based on its awareness of the wholeness of you and your relationship to everyOne. Your ego takes a more limited and defensive posture. It just wants to survive, separate and apart from all others. And, unlike the soul, it wants it *now*—instant ego gratification. In those instances, when you can become the *watcher* of you, and hear this inner dialogue, you are more apt to be guided by your soul, with integrity as the standard by which your choice is measured.

Tune In to Love and Fear

As the ever-present debate between soul and ego ensues, pay special attention to the emotional energy that enters the fray as *love* and *fear*. You can sense these two emotional forms in your body, thanks to the natural soul-body connection when your awareness is attuned to emotion. There is a constant interplay between love and fear as they show up in most every life event, frivolous or grand, given that *emotion* is the universal movement of One in the HD. It is not surprising that the soul speaks fluent love, whereas the ego spews fear. Tuning in to these conflicting emotions can help you moderate the debate between soul and ego and ultimately guide you toward a more integrative choice. It is worth returning to the description of love and fear from Chapter 3 to become fluent in their language.

Love creates, includes, integrates, collaborates, heals, eases, accepts, compromises, embraces, shares, reveals, expands, sends out, stays, engages, opens up, and sees possibilities. Love is patient and kind.

Fear destroys, divides, separates, competes, harms, forces, rejects, confronts, recoils, hoards, hides, contracts, draws in, flees, disengages, shuts down, and sees limitations. Fear is impatient and cruel.

Heed the Whisper

Throughout this journey, I have mentioned the truth being "whispered" to you in songs, stories, nature, spontaneous events, chance encounters, and conventional wisdom of the HD. Consider this new example: One day you are bored, so you begin channel surfing. You land on a documentary about a new vacation "hot spot" that piques your interest. You have never visited this place, but you are intrigued. At the time, you have no plans for a vacation trip but somehow this place seems compelling. For a while, you find it crossing your mind often throughout the day, but then you forget about it. A few weeks later, you are paging through a magazine and turn to a travel ad offering deals to the same destination. What a coincidence! Then, the following week, you run into a former co-worker who casually mentions that she has just returned from that same place. You decide to take advantage of the deal in the magazine and make the trip. While on the trip, you meet someone special and form a meaningful, lifelong relationship that you would otherwise have missed.

While such events appear to be random and coincidental, they reflect the balance, order, and harmony characteristic of the absolute. Each event arises as an *opportunity* in The Creation Cycle, whispered to you for your understanding, choice, and action, with the intention of discreetly pointing you in the *perfect* direction. Pay attention. Heed the whisper. Believe it or not, everyOne conspires to gracefully nurture and guide you along the way in the human dimension. When you can recognize these whispers as signposts, and follow them in your daily life, you are guided toward the experience of greater well-being.

Carl Jung, the founder of analytical psychology, called these patterns of events *synchronicity*, and described them as meaningful coincidences, occurring with no apparent causal relationship, yet seeming to be related. He believed that, just as events may be connected by causality, they may also be connected by meaning. While one does not cause the other, there is still a significant relationship between them. The concept of synchronicity supported Jung's theory of a single unconscious mind shared by all human beings, which he called the *collective unconscious*, a construct which sounds very much like the truth of everyOne and the absolute.

4. Accept What Happens

There is a powerful truth conveyed in this traditional Taoist parable about a farmer and his horse. It is a beautiful lesson on creating grace in your life.

> There was an old farmer who lived in the country with his son and their horse. One day the old man entered his beautiful stallion in a local show and won first prize. Hearing of the farmer's good fortune, his neighbor stopped by to congratulate him, to which the old man responded, "Who knows what is good and what is bad?"
>
> The news of the prizewinning stallion spread through the region and the next day some thieves came and stole the farmer's horse. His neighbor returned to commiserate with the farmer, but the old man simply responded with, "Who knows what is good and what is bad?"
>
> A few days later, the spirited stallion escaped from the thieves, joined a herd of wild mares, and returned with the mares to the farm. The neighbor, seeing all the horses from next door, called upon the farmer to share his joy, but all the farmer said was, "Who knows what is good and what is bad?"

The following day, while trying to break in one of the new mares, the farmer's son was thrown and broke his leg. The neighbor, who witnessed this event, rushed over to share the farmer's sorrow, but the old man's attitude remained the same as before. The following week the army passed through the countryside, forcibly conscripting all able-bodied men as soldiers for the war. They did not take the farmer's son, because he was on crutches and unable to walk. At last, the neighbor thought to himself, "Who knows what is good and what is bad?" and realized that the old farmer must be a Taoist sage.

Suspend the "Good-Bad" Polarity

Admit it. You are hooked on labeling most events in life somewhere on the line between the points of "good" and "bad." It is an exhausting habit that adds tremendous worry and stress to your experience. But labeling an event "good" or "bad" is quite simply a *choice* to *understand* that event in a particular way. In The Creation Cycle, every moment of life is simply an opportunity entering your awareness and awaiting your understanding and choice. From the absolute perspective, there are no "good" or "bad" opportunities in The Creation Cycle. All opportunities are created equal. They are *equal opportunity* opportunities.

Moreover, every opportunity arrives at your awareness as the product of countless relationships, woven together by everyOne to form the everyOne channel—that is, the human dimension. You and everyOne construct these relationships with the choices you make. Every opportunity arrives exactly as you and everyOne have created it to be, regardless of whether at first it seems "bad" or "good."

Suffering Is Optional

Still, you might ask: If it is true that you and everyOne are the expression of perfect and true, how could anything ever go wrong here in the human dimension? In truth, from the perspective of the absolute, it does not. But from the standpoint of the HD, it seems like trouble awaits you at every turn. *Trouble,* in most instances, means some measure of suffering or lack of well-being due to adversities such as:

- Fires, floods, tsunamis, earthquakes, and other natural disasters
- Abject poverty, hunger, and famine
- Refugee displacement and perilous escapes to safety
- Cancer and other debilitating and life-threatening diseases
- Loss of job, home, and financial security
- Mental and emotional distress, depression, and anxiety
- Ultimately, death

The idea of suffering, or lack of anything, is incompatible with the absolute. From an absolute point of view, there is no suffering, and nothing is lacking, because everything is *perfect* and *true.* Of course, this is all fine and dandy for the absolute, but here you are with your two feet firmly planted in the more precarious human dimension where perfect and true is experienced only by means of polarity. The struggle is real in the HD.

There is a popular truism attributed to renowned Japanese writer, Haruki Murakami, which says: "Pain is inevitable. Suffering is optional."[42] This nugget of wisdom relates to the *First Noble Truth* of Buddhism, which says that life is inevitably filled with *dukkha. Dukkha* was originally translated as *suffering,* but is now interpreted by scholars to mean *unsatisfactoriness* of all sorts: *unhappiness, distress, disease, misfortune, adversity, disorder, chaos, unrest, etc.* While it is true that there are unsatisfactory conditions in the human dimension that might be *painful* for you, in the end, it is your *resistance* to these conditions, in place of your *acceptance,* that produces your suffering. To be clear,

---

42. Haruki Murakami, *What I Talk About When I Talk About Running: A Memoir,* (National Geographic Books, 2009), VII.

accepting life's dukkha does not mean you approve of it, but that you merely acknowledge such conditions exist. Upon accepting that an unsatisfactory condition has entered your awareness as an opportunity, you are empowered to understand it, and choose whether to suffer through it or set it aside and create the condition anew. The Creation Cycle is a powerful and fail-safe tool for creating change. To interject a little "tough love" here, you can wallow in self-pity (suffering) or get on with your life. The choice of what to do next is always yours, but know that it can look like this:

- First, pause, and view the situation as it is presented to you by the *this-that* of polarity in the human dimension. In other words, pain (unsatisfactoriness) arises only in opposition to comfort (satisfactoriness), therefore comfort is most certainly available to you.

- Next, intentionally see the situation as an opportunity entering your awareness in The Creation Cycle.

- Then, use this opportunity to apply your understanding of what you have remembered here about *who you are, where you came from,* and *why you are here.* You are One with the ability to create as you choose!

- Finally, as One, choose what action you will take next.

It is just that simple. To accept what happens does not mean rolling over and acquiescing to whatever happens. Acceptance does not ask you to abdicate from continuing to create. On the contrary, it asks for your next choice, given the opportunity presented to you in The Creation Cycle. But should you choose *not* to follow these steps, do some soul-searching as to *why*. By soul-searching I mean, quite literally, listen for your soul's voice in making your choice. It is likely to be found slugging it out with your ego.

Tame the Ego

The ego is a fascinating beast. Its entire existence is predicated on making you forget who you are, and blinding you to the truth that you are One. If it is successful, the ego gets to run the show. When the ego believes it is threatened, which is most of the time, it mobilizes an attack or defense, especially when the threat originates from another ego. You have witnessed this regular scenario play out everywhere—the bedroom and the boardroom, the streets and the temples, the office and the classroom, the dining table and the dressing table, the battlefield and the playing field, and so on. In truth, the drama of "battling egos" is the cause of most suffering, unease, and forgetting who we truly are in the human dimension. With your ego in charge, you are provided with dreadful, life-altering polarities such as: *us-them, good-bad, pleasure-pain, gain-loss, reward-punishment, righteousness-sin, heaven-hell,* and *absolution-judgment.* Clearly, this is how things get messy in the HD.

The subject of the ego is a good place to revisit the "d-word." For most people, death has a bad reputation. To the fragile ego, it is the ultimate threat and is seen as both an ending and a failure. This limited view of death is the product of the ego's confinement to your mind. The ego is quite literally *narrow-minded.* Neither your soul nor your body can relate to the concept of death. They view death merely as the natural *reformation* of the energy of your human form, which is necessary to exit the human dimension and return to One and the absolute. With your form's departure, the illusion of polarity disappears and the *ego* dissolves. With no ego, suffering ends and you are, again, One with the absolute from where you came.

If you were *only* your ego, some degree of unsatisfactoriness, even contempt, toward other people and things, as well as death, might make sense. But now, by grace, you can remember that you are *not* your ego. Your ego is merely another product of polarity in the human dimension and, to the extent you can call it *real* at all, it exists only in the part of you that is your mind. As One, you are far greater than your ego can conceive. And although the ego is not going away, you can tame it by simply being a witness to its antics, accepting its inevitability, and, ultimately, choosing with integrity.

5. Take Responsibility

Upon fully embracing the truth of who you are, you gain precious insight into the true structure, mechanism, and even theology of the whole human dimension. You become keenly aware that everything you experience in the HD is of your creation. *Everything.* Thus, if you have ever searched for a god, look no further. And if you have never believed in a god, now you have a new alternative to consider. But here is the dilemma: *you* are at the center of it all. It is all about *you*. You are the One creating. Consequently, you are responsible for what you create. Are you ready for that?

"With great power comes great responsibility." This cautionary truism has been uttered countless times throughout the ages by notable thought leaders, such as Luke the Evangelist, Voltaire, Winston Churchill, Franklin Roosevelt, and even Marvel's amazing Spiderman. But when it really comes down to it, not everybody wants to take on the responsibility that comes with great power. Many are thirsty for power but shun the accountability that comes with it.

Interestingly, the word *responsibility* comes from the Latin word *respons*, meaning to *reply* or *answer,* and this is precisely what you do with The Creation Cycle. As the creator, you answer each *opportunity* that enters your awareness with your *choice*, then *act* upon the choice you make. To assume responsibility, then, means to act with the understanding that your choices and actions create your experience. Recognizing this truth is vital to your experience of the HD.

Thoughts, Prayers, and the Wild West

Avoiding responsibility for what we create in the human dimension is an everyday occurrence that comes at a great price. For example, in May 2022, news headlines reported yet another gun violence incident in Uvalde, Texas in which twenty-one people were killed by gunfire in an elementary school. The reaction was predictable: *thoughts and prayers.* This common chorus is indicative of the true underlying problem that has long afflicted the human dimension. By neglecting to embrace who we truly are, we ignore our responsibility, first by relying too heavily on our thinking minds (and their egos) in our choices, then praying to a disembodied higher power to fix a problem we created in the first place. The Uvalde tragedy, and all the prior and subsequent school shootings, are perfect examples of the cost of forgetting the truth about who we are. Collectively they indict us with a version of insanity often attributed to Einstein: "doing the same thing over and over, expecting a different result."

Following this Texas shooting, actor Matthew McConaughey, who hails from Uvalde, offered this insight on Twitter: "We have tragically proven that we are failing to be responsible for the rights our freedoms grant us."[43] He is right. In this shameful situation and countless others, amidst all the *thinking* of thoughts, no one *thinks* to ask the truly vital questions:

What role did I play creating the opportunity for this shooting?
In what way did my choices and actions impact the awareness and understanding of the perpetrator?
How can I choose differently in the future to prevent such misery?

---

43. "Here's what Matthew McConaughey said about the shooting in his hometown." NPR. May 25, 2022. Accessed February 19, 2023. https://www.npr.org/2022/05/25/1101168374/matthew-mcconaughey-uvalde-school-shooting

Is it time to take a more holistic approach to the solution?

Do I truly care enough to make the effort?

The Uvalde case is simple. Except for hunting guns, we create guns for the sole purpose of injuring and killing people. Of course, people are injured and killed in other ways too, but guns are made expressly for this purpose. Why, then, are we surprised when they are used as intended? In our failing to remember who we truly are, we have not only created a new "Wild West" of opportunity to kill other people, but the perfect tool with which to do it. Yet we are still shocked and require more "thought" on the subject while we pray.

Who is the divine being we must appeal to for help here? It is *you*. As One, you are the creator of your experience in the human dimension and, since every creation of yours is an opportunity for another, you help shape the experience of others. We want to believe there is a powerful protector up in the sky to help us. We rally with: "In God we trust" and "Jesus saves." But *you* are the almighty. And *you* are the savior and the fixer. I am sorry if this makes you uncomfortable. But it is the truth. Until we can fully embrace who we are, choose with integrity, and take responsibility for our choices, nothing will change. We need to bring some grace to the fight for our well-being.

I realize this is not what you have been told. You have likely come to accept that you play only a small role, if any, in creating the events that shape your life experience. Franchised religion has sold us on the belief that there is some omnipotent god, juxtaposed to a nefarious devil, who pull the strings in the human dimension. Likewise, the scientific establishment has schooled you with "facts" suggesting that the HD functions like a colossal machine, in which you are merely a cog in the wheel. When pressed for more, these high-handed institutions ask you to have *faith* or *trust the research*. Both have flourished as the self-appointed gatekeepers to our salvation. To placate the masses, they offer us distracting rites and rituals, or the next best techno-gadget, perpetuating the illusion that we are dependent upon them for our rescue. In the end, they obfuscate the truth that you, me, and everyOne are responsible for the choices we make in our collective creation.

That all sounds very dark. But the truth is far brighter. You do not need faith and trust, and you are not powerless. *You are the creator.* By taking responsibility for every phase of The Creation Cycle, you are free to create with integrity. You are the One in charge. It is all about you. Remember this empowering truth about you.

Absolution

On the flip side, you know that you do not always make choices that reflect the integrity of your perfect and true nature. No *One* can. By fully embracing who you are, you are also called upon to remember that you are One, being human. And as a human being amid the constraints of polarity in the human dimension, you must navigate a world of choices between two points. Perhaps foolishly, sometimes unwittingly, and certainly understandably, you choose the point which produces the unsatisfying, even painful, outcome for you or others. This problem is unavoidable.

The answer to this problem, offered by the leaders of the Abrahamic religions, is God's forgiveness. Under this plan, God is imagined to be up there, somewhere, separate and apart from you, with greater power and authority over you, sitting in an exalted position of judgment. When this God forgives you, you are released from the burden of your bad choices and their agonizing outcomes. Naturally, this scheme also implies that this God requires you to behave in a specifically prescribed manner in the HD.

As One, now you can remember the truth that there is no particular behavior prescribed or mandated for you that, if not obeyed, would require any god's forgiveness. There is only the simple truth that when you make choices that reflect the integrity of the whole you, soul-body-mind, you create an experience of contentment and well-being. When your choices do *not* reflect this integrity, you create an experience that lacks contentment and well-being. It is just that simple. You have only the consequences of your choices in The Creation Cycle to deal with.

In the inevitable situations in which your choices lack integrity, rather than seeking forgiveness from some distant, detached deity, *you* are the exact deity from which forgiveness is properly due. *Absolution* from the perfect and true *absolute* seems fitting, does it not? That means *you*! The basis for you forgiving you is your new understanding of the truth about you. Your graceful act of self-compassion and self-absolution serves to rebalance and harmonize the essential parts of you (soul-mind-body) and helps reconcile the paradox of living amid the illusion of the HD within the truth of the absolute.

There is no escaping the truth. Ready or not, it is all about you. As a child of the absolute, the gifts of grace are yours to choose, apply, and enjoy. When you embrace who you are, recognize everyOne, choose with integrity, accept what happens, and take responsibility for what you create, you are renewed and re-created, and the entire community of the human dimension leaps forward, toward its next magnificent expression of the absolute in humanity. This is *what's in it for you.*

Sati Ten: Let It Be

1. Find your seat (refer to Sati One, if needed) and settle in.

2. Start by taking 10 vishama-vritti breaths, where you gently inhale to the count of three and slowly exhale to the count of six, such that your exhale is twice as long as your inhale.

3. Next, with your eyes open or closed, spend a moment taking inventory of whatever is currently passing through your immediate experience. Include the various sights, sounds, smells, body sensations, thoughts, and feelings. These are all the parts of your here and now.

4. Spend about five minutes watching each of these parts of your experience as they enter and exit your awareness, sometimes perhaps lingering a bit, without judgment, as if they were all strangers passing by while you sit on your porch, or a park bench. Simply notice them and let them be.

5. As you notice each, say to yourself silently: "let it be," and move on to the next.

6. Finally, relax your awareness and open your eyes.

This is the practice of equanimity or nonattachment. It helps to promote mental composure, tranquility, and serenity by letting go and accepting what happens. By developing this ability in your meditation seat, you are better equipped to handle difficulties and challenges as they arise in your life. Nonattachment helps you calmly observe all the "passersby" in your here and now without judgment or discomfort, each time cultivating a bit more grace in your experience of life.

Commencement

If you know your reality first,
you will be able to know the reality of the world.
It is a strange thing that most people
do not care to know about their own reality
but are very anxious to know about the reality of the world.
You realize your own Self first and then see
if the world exists independently of you
and is able to come and assert before you its reality or existence.[44]
—From 'Day by Day with Bhagavan' 19-10-45 Morning

BY CHOOSING TO COMPLETE THIS JOURNEY, YOU HAVE BEEN REWARDED with the extraordinary opportunity to remember how perfectly the individual parts come together to tell the whole truth of *who you are, where you came from,* and *why you are here.* Any single part, by itself, might be susceptible to doubt. Their magnificence lies in how they all fit together perfectly and integratively to reveal the truth of it all. (See Figure 20.) *Satyagraha!* You are not asked to have faith, believe in the supernatural, or trust science. You are One. You need only to listen to *you* to remember, firsthand, the long-forgotten truth that you brought with you into this world and accept that you are far grander that you ever imagined.

44. A. Devaraja Mudaliar, *Day by Day: With Bhagavan* (Chennai, India: Nesma Books, 2002), 19-10-45 Morning.

Figure 20
Parts of the Whole

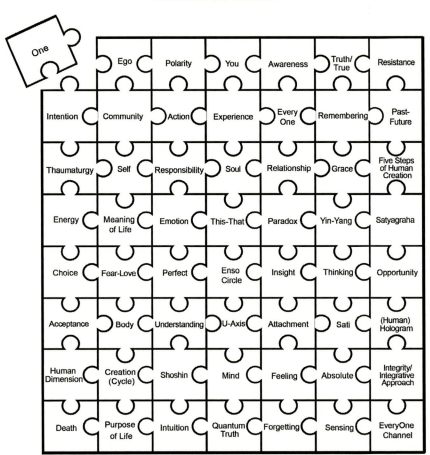

It is decidedly difficult to remember the truth of it all from within the illusion of polarity. The rules and bounds of the human dimension are meant to hide the truth. While this seems unfair, it is not impossible to overcome when you remember how the illusion, itself, fits within the whole truth, and that it is but one tiny speck of it all. But you must be willing to step outside of the illusion, regardless of how alluring it is.

You are not at the end, but at the beginning, of this journey. This is your commencement. For as long as you choose to appear in the human dimension, this tight little theory of everything is here to serve you. Let it be your recharging station, for plugging back in to the perfect and true, remembering the truth when you forget, bringing integrity to your choices, answering your most pressing questions, unraveling life's biggest mysteries, or simply to catch your breath when the human dimension gets to be too much. Thereupon, you may return to the illusion and continue to create the experience of your absolute choosing.

Remember this **Truth:**
Amid the captivating illusion of **Polarity,**
Absolute appears as **One**,
And as **You**, Soul-Body-Mind,
To **Create** and **Experience**
A multitude of **Relationships**
With **Grace.**

References

"Albert Einstein Quotes." Brainy Quote. Accessed February 19, 2023. https://www.brainyquote.com/quotes/albert_einstein_109020

"Anne Lamott Quotes." Goodreads. Accessed February 20, 2023. From *Traveling Mercies: Some Thoughts on Faith*. https://www.goodreads.com/quotes/6476160-i-do-not-at-all-understand-the-mystery-of-grace--only

Barrett, David B., George T. Kurion, and Todd M. Johnson. *World Christian Encyclopedia: A Comparative Survey of Churches and Religions in the Modern World, 2 Volume Set*. USA: Oxford University Press, Second Edition, 2001.

"Being Christian in Western Europe." Pew Research Center. (May 28, 2018). https://www.pewresearch.org/religion/2018/05/29/being-christian-in-western-europe/

Bonewits, Isaac. *Authentic Thaumaturgy*. 2nd ed. Steve Jackson Games, 1998.

Church, Dawson. *Mind to Matter: The Astonishing Science of How Your Brain Creates Material Reality*. Carlsbad: Hay House, 2018.

Clark, Ronald. *Einstein: The Life and Times*. London: Hodder and Stoughton Ltd., 1973.

David Lynch Foundation, "The thing about meditation is, you become more and more you."—David Lynch. Facebook, May 9, 2016. https://www.facebook.com/DavidLynchFoundation/photos/a.175572862467475/1179252585432826/?type=3 de Chardin, P. T. "The Evolution of Chastity," essay in *Toward the Future*. Mariner Books, 2002. [https://archive.org/details/TowardTheFuture/mode/2up?q=someday]

"Forbes Quotes: Thoughts on the Business of Life." Forbes. Accessed February 17, 2023. https://www.forbes.com/quotes/173/

"Here's what Matthew McConaughey said about the shooting in his hometown." NPR. May 25, 2022. Accessed February 19, 2023. https://www.npr.org/2022/05/25/1101168374/matthew-mcconaughey-uvalde-school-shooting

Herguth, Robert. "Face to Faith, Episode 5 Jim Lovell." *Face to Faith*. Audio podcast. March 23, 2018. Chicago Sun-Times. https://chicago.suntimes.com https://soundcloud.com/user-485806571-926828048/face-to-faith-episode-5-jim-lovell

"I am Justice: Clear, Impartial." Poet Seers. Accessed Feruary 20, 2023. Trans. by Stephen Mitchell, based on The Bhagavad Gita an interlinear translation by Winthrop Sargeant. https://www.poetseers.org/spiritual-and-devotional-poets/india/bhagavad-gita/i-am-justice/

"Interview with Bhikkhu Bodhi: Translator for the Buddha." Inquiring Mind. Spring 2006. Vol. 22, No. 2, http://www.inquiringmind.com/article/2202_w_bodhi-interview-with-bhikkhu-bodhi-translator-for-the-buddha/.

"I Sing the Body Electric by Walt Whitman." Poetry Foundation. Accessed February 19, 2023. https://www.poetryfoundation.org/poems/45472/i-sing-the-body-electric

Langley, Noel; Florence Ryerson; and Edgar Allen Woolf. "The Wizard of Oz." Film script, 1939.

Lin, Derek. n.d. "Tao Te Ching Online Translation." Taoism.net. Accessed February 18, 2023. https://taoism.net/tao-te-ching-online-translation/.

"(The) Mind of Absolute Trust by Seng-Ts'an." Poetry Chaikhana: Sacred Poetry from Around the World. Accessed February 19, 2023. https://www.poetry-chaikhana.com/Poets/S/SengTsan/Mindof/index.html

Mitchell, David. *Cloud Atlas*. Random House Trade. 2004.

Mudaliar, A. Devaraja. *Day by Day: With Bhagavan*. Chennai, India: Nesma Books. 2002.

Murakami, Haruki. *What I Talk About When I Talk About Running: A Memoir*. National Geographic Books, 2009.

"Newton's Laws of Motion." NASA Glenn Research Center. Accessed February 18, 2023. https://www1.grc.nasa.gov/beginners-guide-to-aeronautics/newtons-laws-of-motion/

"Nikola Tesla Quotes." Goodreads. Accessed February 20, 2023. https://www.goodreads.com/quotes/1133528-every-living-being-is-an-engine-geared-to-the-wheelwork

Nin, Anais. *Seduction of the Minotaur*. Athens, GA: Ohio University Press.1961.

Nisbett, R. E. & K. Peng (1999). "Culture, dialectics, and reasoning about contradiction." *American Psychologist, 54*(9), 741-754. https://doi.org/10.1037/0003-066x.54.9.741

O'Donohue, John. *Wisdom from the Celtic World: A Gift-Boxed Trilogy of Celtic Wisdom*. Audio CD. Sounds True; Unabridged edition. July 29, 2005.

"Our self (Soul) is maya . . ." AZ Quotes. Accessed February 19, 2023. https://www.azquotes.com/quote/535597

"Pierre Teilhard de Chardin Quotes." Goodreads. Accessed February 20, 2023. https://www.goodreads.com/quotes/21263-we-are-not-human-beings-having-a-spiritual-experience-we

"Sixteen Going on Seventeen (Reprise) Lyrics." The Rogers & Hammerstein Organization. Accessed February 19, 2023. https://rodgersandhammerstein.com/song/the-sound-of-music/sixteen-going-on-seventeen-reprise/

"Summary of Bhagavad Gita, Chapter 7, Part 3." The Art of Living. Accessed February 19, 2023. https://www.artofliving.org/wisdom/summary-bhagavad-gita-chapter7-part3

Suzuki, Shunryu. *Zen Mind, Beginners Mind.* Boulder, Colorado: Shambhala Publications, Inc., 2020.

Tolle, Eckhart. *A New Earth: Awakening to Your Life's Purpose.* Penguin Life, 2008.

Walsch, Neale Donald. *Conversations with God—Book 1.* New York: Putnam's Sons, 1995.

"What Makes Me." The Brain with Dr. David Eagleman. 2015. Directed by Dan Clifton, Catherine Gale, and Johanna Woolford Gibbon. Aired October 21, 2015, on PBS.

"What You Resist Persists." *Well Being.* September 6, 2019. Accessed February 19, 2023. https://www.wellbeing.com.au/wild/what-you-resist-persists-10-ways-overcome-resistance

"When Americans Say They Believe in God, What do They Mean?" Pew Research Center. (April 25, 2018). https://www.pewresearch.org/religion/2018/04/25/when-americans-say-they-believe-in-god-what-do-they-mean/

Wilson, E.O. *Consilience: The Unity of Knowledge.* New York: Alfred S. Knopf, 2000.

"Worldwide, Many See Belief in God As Essential to Morality." Pew Research Center. (March 13, 2014). https://www.pewresearch. org/global/2014/03/13/worldwide-many-see-belief-in-god-as-essential-to-morality/

"Yanni Quotes." Goodreads. Accessed February 10, 2023. https:// www.goodreads.com/quotes/1226561-creativity-is-an-inherent-human-quality-of-the-highest-order

Glossary

Absolute—The *metaphysical* (*beyond* the physical), *metapolar* (*beyond* polarity) realm which precedes, encompasses, and transcends humanity and the **human dimension**, with the defining qualities of (1) **perfect** (complete, fulfilled, and utterly evolved) and (2) **true**. Could be described as a state of being, another dimension or plane, an omnipresence, or even the container or source of all that is.

Acceptance—Adopting the **absolute** perspective that there are no "good" or "bad" opportunities in **The Creation Cycle**. Every moment of life is simply an **opportunity** entering your **awareness** and awaiting your **understanding** and **choice**. This practice includes: (1) avoiding the labeling of a person, thing, or event as "good" or "bad," (2) understanding that suffering is optional, and (3) taming the ego.

Action—One of the five phases of **The Creation Cycle**; action is your **choice** set into motion, powered by the **energy** of your **intention**. Action propels whatever **you** choose out into the **human dimension** as a current of **energy** in the frequency of a newly created form, movement, or possibility, becoming available as an **opportunity** for others. Some actions are directed *outward,* toward other people or things, whereas other actions are directed *inward,* like your **choices** about how to **think** or **feel**.

Attachment—One of two expressions of **intention** (the other is **resistance**), in which **you** extend your attention toward another point on a line of **polarity** and say: "yes." Attachment extends toward and latches on to something, such as a form, object, feeling, or human being, and "holds on" or "pulls" it toward **you**.

Awareness—One of the five phases of **The Creation Cycle**; your antenna for detecting the energies of *form, movement,* and *possibility* in the **human dimension**; includes the channels of **sensing, emotion,** and **intuition**. Awareness is how **you** take it all in. In other words, it is your *reception*.

Body—Part of the soul-body-mind **hologram** appearing as **you** in the **human dimension**, formed with **polarity**, along with the **mind**, at Step 2 of the **Five Steps of Human Creation**. One half of the **soul's** expression as two, *material* (**body**) and the *conscious* (**mind**). Your **body** is your instrument for interacting and relating with all the other bodies and **form** in the HD, both as a *receiver* for your experience and a *tool* for your creative expression. Just like your hands both **experience** and **create** for **you** in the **HD**, so does your body **experience** and **create** for **One**. In **truth**, your body is the hand of **One** in the **HD**.

Choice (Choose)—One of the five phases of **The Creation Cycle**; *choice* always follows **understanding** in **The Creation Cycle**. It is your personal stamp and ultimate decree as to what **you** will **create**. Ultimately, your choice determines what **action you** will take in the next step of **The Creation Cycle**.

Community—Human beings coming together to **create** change with an **awareness** of our **relationship** to, or Oneness with, all others. Community begins with the **understanding** that our entire **experience** emerges from the **absolute**, the single, whole, unified, ubiquitous, source of **perfect and true**.

Creation Cycle (Creation)—The five-phase process of creation for everything appearing in the **human dimension**. The phases of The Creation Cycle are pictured below. Each phase has a unique part to play in this infinite and eternal circle of life. Creation is the **meaning of life**.

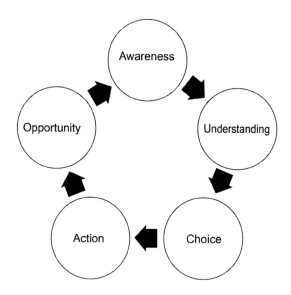

Death—The **Five Steps of Human Creation** in reverse. Rather than extending outward into the **human dimension**, the energies of **body** and **mind** withdraw back toward the soul, which then reunites with **One** and, ultimately, rejoins the infinite and eternal **absolute**.

Ego—The "me first" aspect of the human **mind** established in Step 4 of the **Five Steps of Human Creation**. Ego is an expression of the **self** in the **HD, created** with **polarity**, masking the **truth** that **you** are **One**. Ego sees your **self** as being apart from (instead of a part of) the **absolute**, separate from all that surrounds **you** in the HD and, different than **One**. With the ego, we begin to *compete* instead of *collaborate*. We are not competitive by nature, because our nature is **absolute** so, in **truth**, there is nothing and no one to compete against. But the ego is competitive by design. Its survival is predicated on its differentiation from, and triumph over, all other egos.

Emotion—One of three channels of **awareness**; attuned to the energetic pulsing, vibrating movement of **One** in the **human dimension**. With emotion, your **soul** reminds **you** of your close connection to **One** and tries its best to translate that enormous **truth** into the finite realm of the **HD** through your **body**. Emotion is **understood** in the **human dimension** by **feeling**, and with the **polarity** of **love-fear**.

Energy (energetic)—The forceful expression of the **absolute**, and the source and basis of all that we **experience**, and might possibly **experience**, in the **human dimension**; sometimes called *life force, chi, prana, spirit*, and *elan*.

Enso Circle—Also known as the Affinity Circle, Zen Circle, and Circle of Togetherness. The ensō is painted with a single, fluid brushstroke. Once it is drawn, it is not altered in any way, in order to honor the singular, present moment in which the mind frees the **body** to **create**. Here it represents the circular trajectory, or "truth loop," of **creation** and **experience**, which go hand-in-hand, one always following the other. **You create** your **experience**, then **you experience** your **creation**. **You** go around and around in this true circle of life.

EveryOne—Each and every **One** in the **human dimension**.

EveryOne Channel—Energetic network or "chat room" where **everyOne** and all the stuff of the **human dimension** are "tuned in" and connected. This common channel is what allows **you** to mix, mingle, touch, collaborate, plan, organize, share experiences, and generally relate to all **others** in the **HD**. The vast network of **relationships** that provides **you** and **everyOne** with **opportunities** in **The Creation Cycle** and shapes your **experience** of the **HD**. The **human dimension** is **truly** the **everyOne** channel.

Experience—The **purpose of life**: observing, encountering, or undergoing whatever processes, events, or things **you choose** to **create** in the **human dimension**.

Feeling—One of three means of **understanding**; this is the **understanding** of **emotion**, in which **body** and **soul** work together to comprehend the prickly **relationship** between **love and fear**, the two polar opposite expressions of **emotion** in the **human dimension.**

Five Steps of Human Creation—See the illustration below:

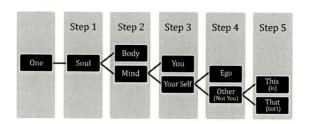

Form—Energetic configurations, or patterns, in the **human dimension experienced** with **polarity,** Includes all *solid* or *material* form (i.e., book, tree, car, people), *gaseous* form (i.e., oxygen, helium, carbon dioxide), liquid form (i.e., pools, ponds, oceans), sound form (i.e., music, talking, birds chirping), *light* form (i.e., lamplight, rainbow, candlelight), and so on. All form originates from formlessness, or **taiji.**

Grace—The event of the **absolute** gently piercing the illusion of the **HD** with the qualities of **perfect and true,** nudging **you** toward living as **One**—a fully **integrated** being of **soul-body-mind.** Simply put, *grace* is the "feel good" **experience** of the **absolute** in the HD.

Hologram—A three-dimensional image formed by a coherent source of light **energy.**

Human dimension (or "HD")—The world, or realm, inhabited by human beings; where we focus our attention and **energy;** includes planet Earth and all other heavenly bodies within our **awareness;** encompasses what we **experience** as *physical* objects and beings, and nonphysical or *metaphysical* **energy** that surrounds us, such as light and sound. Called *human* dimension because it is **created** by human beings.

Human geometry—The mathematical basis for all material **form** in the **human dimension**, based on points, lines, solids, space, the traditional geometric axes (x, y, and z), and incorporating the **u-axis**. The simple, mathematical foundation of the **human dimension.**

Insight—One of three means of **understanding** in which **soul** and **mind** team up to decipher the limitless possibilities of the **absolute** entering your **awareness** as **intuition**; uses the **polarity** of **past-future** to separate and sort out events and all manner of **form** in the **HD**, giving each one meaning by comparing it to all others. Insight imparts **vision**, so your **mind** can more easily reconcile and assimilate all the possibilities and mysteries of the **absolute** universe from within the limited framework of **polarity.**

Integrative approach—A "parts to whole" path to the **truth** in which **soul, body**, and **mind** work together, or *integrate,* to arrive at an **understanding**, i.e., **remembering;** and an approach to **truth** that incorporates the established views of many disciplines.

Integrity/integrate(-d)—The state of being whole, unified, complete, and as one; to make whole.

Intention—The powerful creative **energy** behind every choice **you** make in **The Creation Cycle**. With your intention you shape the **energies** of **form**, *movement,* and *possibility* that have entered your **awareness** through **sensing, emotion**, and **intuition**, and which **you** have come to **understand** with **thought, feeling**, and **insight**. When **you choose**, the creative **energy** of your intention turns its attention to, and extends toward, a **form**, movement, or possibility, annexing it into your **experience** in the **human dimension**. Intention is expressed in one of two ways: **attachment** or **resistance**.

Intuition—One of three channels of **awareness**; this is the channel of all human possibility. When **awareness** comes through intuition, your **soul** teams up with your **mind** to reveal the vast array of possibilities for **you** and all of humanity.

Love-fear—One of The Major **Polarities** of the HD; these are the two polarities that enable us to **experience** the **energetic** movement (vibration or pulsation) of **One** in the **HD**.

Meaning of Life—The meaning of life is, simply, **creation**, as defined by **The Creation Cycle**. **Creation** is "what's happening" in the **human dimension** and nothing more.

Mind—Part of the **soul-body-mind hologram** appearing as **you** in the **human dimension**, formed with polarity, along with the **body**, at Step 2 of the **Five Steps of Human Creation**, responsible for establishing your identity in the **human dimension** and the **ego**, which serves to perpetuate the illusion of your separation from all **others**.

One—The outward, active, and revealed expression of the absolute in the **human dimension**, as **you**, in the **form** of a three-part **energetic hologram** of **soul, body**, and **mind**. One originates from the **absolute** and enters the **human dimension** as **you** with the **Five Steps of Human Creation**.

Opportunity—One of the five phases of **The Creation Cycle**; it is the situation in which **you** find yourself or the *conditions* that provide your **awareness**. It is the hand **you** have been dealt to play and create with. Opportunity asks the question "what will **you create?**," which is answered by your **choice**. Also, the creative product of all human beings universally and eternally in the **human dimension**. It is the creative masterpiece of **form**, movement, and possibility of **everyOne**, throughout all human history, **created** together by our collective **awareness, understanding, choice,** and **action**.

Other—That which **you experience** in the illusion of the **human dimension** as *not* **you**. Whereas, in **truth**, there is no other.

Paradox—A condition wherein two seemingly opposite ideas or conditions co-exist.

Past-future—One of The Major **Polarities** of the HD; this **polarity** serves as two reference points for our **minds** to evaluate and comprehend the infinite possibilities from which we may **experience** the present moment.

Perfect and true—(1) perfect (complete, fulfilled, and utterly evolved) and (2) **true** (constant and constructive).

Polarity—The means for **creating** and **experiencing** the **human dimension**; defined by its five basic elements:

1. A thing may enter your **awareness** only in the presence of its opposite.
2. A thing is **understood** only by comparing it to that which it is not. It is the relative difference, or *value*, between the two that allows **you** to know both.
3. *Only* through polarity may **you** have **experiences** in the HD.
4. Polarity is an illusion because, by its own definition, it exists only relative to that which it is not.
5. That which is *not* polarity is ***absolute***.

Purpose of life—To **experience** whatever **you choose** to **create**.

Quantum truth—The **truth** that your **body** and everything you **experience** as material in the **HD** are **forms** of vibrating **energy**, appearing within a common, slow, and dense frequency range, as demonstrated by quantum physics. More specifically:

*   materialism, objective reality, and particle theory are increasingly being replaced by consciousness, observer-based reality, and wave theory.

*   wave theory, at its core, has shown that what really *is* is **energy**, behaving as waves, not particles or matter.

*   the **energy** waves surrounding **you** in the **HD** are shaped by your **relationship** to them throughout the five steps of **The Creation Cycle**, most notably, the **intention** of your **choice**.

As such, these **energy** waves are part of your identity. **You** are **one** with them.

- Bell's theorem and the Aspect-Gröblacher experiments have shown the non-locality of reality, meaning that **you** do not **create** the **human dimension** alone. **You** do it in concert with all other human beings—as **One**.

Reason(-ing)—The engine of **thinking**; sometimes called *critical thinking*.

Relationship (lines)—In **human geometry**, a line representing both the difference, and value, between two points (i.e. objects, people, ideas, qualities, etc.), as well as an energetic link that binds them together. The four primary types of **relationships** in the human dimension are between:

- the **absolute** and the **human dimension**
- **soul, body,** and **mind**
- **you** and your **self**
- **you** and all **other forms**

Remember(-ing)—The process of recognizing a vital, but forgotten, **truth,** arising from a renewed **awareness** of how its integral parts relate to the whole.

Resistance—One of two expressions of **intention** (the other is *attachment*), in which **you** reject or dismiss a thing and push it away. With resistance, **you** also direct and extend your attention toward another point on a line of **polarity**, but **you** say: "no."

Responsibility—Fully embracing the **truth** of who **you** are, acting with **insight** into the **true** structure, mechanism, and even theology of the whole **human dimension**, such that **you** are keenly **aware** that everything **you** experience in the **human dimension** is of **your creation**. **You** are the **One creating**. Consequently, **you** are both causative and accountable for what **you create**.

Sati—Pali and Sanskrit word translated as "mindfulness," derived from *sarati*, meaning "to **remember**." Used here to denote mindfulness exercises at the end of each chapter.

Satyagraha—A Sanskrit word formed from *satya* (truth) and *agraha* (insistence) which has come to mean "**truth** force," denoting the act of being compelled by the utter force of **truth** to reconsider existing thought patterns and view certain aspects of your life very differently.

Self—A *self* emerges when an individual becomes **aware** of its own existence. Your *self* is not **you** at all, but the product of **you** becoming **aware** of and relating to **you**. Your *self* emerges in the part of **you** that is your **mind** at Step 3 of the **Five Steps of Human Creation**. One's self is the **soul** of every human being, which serves as the mirror for **One** to **experience One** with **polarity**. The **soul** is **created** in Step 1 of the **Five Steps of Human Creation**.

Sensing—One of three channels of **awareness** in which **body** "picks up" or "tunes into" the unique **energetic** sub-frequencies of **form**: *light, sound, solid matter, flavor,* and *odor,* using the five senses: *sight, hearing, touch, taste, and smell* (light via sight, sound via hearing, solid matter via touch, and so on). This information is shared with your **mind**.

Shoshin—A Zen Buddhism term meaning "beginner's mind," denoting an open-mind or receptive point of view that is open to possibilities.

Soul—Part of the **soul-body-mind hologram** appearing as **you** in the **human dimension**, formed in Step 1 of the **Five Steps of Human Creation**. Your soul is the first and original **polarity** of your being in the **HD**, the core of your being and the essence of who **you** are. Through your soul, you are never *apart* from, and always *a part* of, **One**. And through your soul, all that is **One** is also available to **you**.

Taiji—The state of undifferentiated and infinite potential, the oneness of all things before **polarity** arises, and the **absolute** source of all human **experience.**

Thaumaturgy—According to the notable pagan author, Isaac Bonewits, in his book *Authentic Thaumaturgy,* "the art and science of 'wonder working;' using magic to actually change things in the physical world." Practitioners are called *thaumaturgists, conjurers,* or *wonderworkers.* Comes from the Greek word *thaumatourgos,* composed from *thauma* (miracle) and *ergon* (work).

Thinking—One of three means of **understanding**; evaluating the various ***this-that*** **relationships** among the **energetic forms** of the **HD** (objects, people, symbols, images, colors, sounds, odors, words, and numbers), which enter your sensory **awareness,** and arriving at an **understanding** by applying *reasoning.*

This-that—One of The Major **Polarities** of the HD; similar to **yin-yang,** but not as all-encompassing; pertains specifically to all **form** in the **human dimension, experienced** through contrasting polar opposites, beginning with the two fundamentally distinct **forms** of **body** (*material form*) and **mind** (*conscious form*). The examples of this **polarity** go on *ad infinitum* to include light-dark, high-low, left-right, fast-slow, loud-quiet, smooth-rough, fragrant-stenchy, sweet-savory, etc. and essentially all **polarities** that define **form** of the **HD.**

(True) human anatomy—The **energetic hologram** of **soul, body,** and **mind** that comprises every human being.

Truth/true—That which is both: (1) *constant* (always, universal, infinite, and eternal; has no beginning or end; simply "is," always has been, and always will be.), and (2) *constructive* (the elemental, underlying organizational principle, or *construct,* of all that is; essential foundation and structural order).

U-axis—In **human geometry**, a fourth geometric axis, joining the conventional 3-D axes of *x, y,* and *z,* to convey that all the **form** in the **human dimension** arises from the geometric *point,* or *point of view,* that is *you.*

Understanding—One of the five phases of **The Creation Cycle**; your *evaluation* or *interpretation* of **awareness**. With your understanding **you** process, sort out, and assign meaning to the **energy** received through your **awareness** using **polarity**. The three *means* of understanding are **thinking, feeling**, and **insight.**

Vision—An instantaneous *seeing* and *knowing* that can occur while **understanding** with **intuition**. With vision, your **mind** can more readily accept and assimilate all the possibilities and mysteries of the **absolute** from within the limited framework of **polarity**.

Yin-yang—One of The Major **Polarities** of the **HD**; the instance or expression of *taiji* (formlessness) as all **form** and phenomena with **polarity** in the **human dimension**. It is the *mother-father* of all **polarities** and one of four significant **polarities** depicting the dual, or *polar,* nature of life in the **human dimension**. *Yin* represents the receptive, inward, tranquil, and passive expressions of yin-yang, whereas *yang* exhibits the projective, outward, restless, and active qualities. Examples are birth and death, fire and water, male and female, day and night, work and play, conflict and resolve, sleeping and waking.

You—The outward, active, and revealed expression of the **absolute** in the **human dimension** as a three-part **energetic hologram of soul, body**, and **mind**; and the culmination of the **Five Steps of Human Creation.**

INDEX